# Ultimate skits

## 20 Parables for Driving Home Your Point

# Flagship church resources

*from* Group Publishing

## *Innovations From Leading Churches*

**Flagship Church Resources** are your shortcut to innovative and effective leadership ideas. You'll find ideas for every area of church leadership including pastoral ministry, adult ministry, youth ministry, and children's ministry.

**Flagship Church Resources** are created by the leaders of thriving, dynamic, and trend-setting churches around the country. These nationally recognized teaching churches host regional leadership conferences and are respected by other pastors and church leaders because their approaches to ministry are so effective. These flagship church resources reveal the proven ideas, programs, and principles that these churches have put into practice.

**Flagship Church Resources** currently available:

- *Doing Life With God*
- *Doing Life With God 2*
- *The Visual Edge:*
  *Compelling Video Connectors for Your Worship Experience*
- *Mission-Driven Worship:*
  *Helping Your Changing Church Celebrate God*
- *An Unstoppable Force:*
  *Daring to Become the Church God Had in Mind*
- *A Follower's Life:*
  *12 Group Studies on What It Means to Walk With Jesus*
- *Leadership Essentials for Children's Ministry*
- *Keeping Your Head Above Water:*
  *Refreshing Insights for Church Leadership*
- *Seeing Beyond Church Walls:*
  *Action Plans for Touching Your Community*
- *unLearning Church:*
  *Just When You Thought You Had Leadership All Figured Out!*

*With more to follow!*

# Ultimate skits

## 20 Parables for Driving Home Your Point

Bryan Belknap

**Flagship church resources**
*from* Group Publishing

# Dedication

*I dedicate this book to Todd Cook at Hoffmantown West for first encouraging me to write skits, to Mosaic for performing them, to Group Workcamps for using them, and to Group Publishing, Inc., for printing them. Most of all, thanks to Jesus for the inspiration and to my bride, Jill, for always listening.*

## Ultimate Skits: 20 Parables for Driving Home Your Point

Copyright © 2002 Bryan Belknap

Visit our Web site: **www.grouppublishing.com**
Visit Mosaic's Web site: **www.mosaic.org**

### Credits
Author: Bryan Belknap
Editor: Kelli B. Trujillo
Creative Development Editor: Amy Simpson
Chief Creative Officer: Joani Schultz
Copy Editor: Betty Taylor
Art Director: Kari K. Monson
Computer Graphic Artist: Stephen Beer
Illustrator: Matt Wood
Production Manager: Dodie Tipton

### Library of Congress Cataloging-in-Publication Data
Belknap, Bryan.
  Ultimate skits : 20 parables for driving home your point / Bryan Belknap
      p. cm.
Includes indexes.
   ISBN 0-7644-2354-1 (pbk. : alk. paper)
  1.   Drama in Christian education.   I. Title.
BV1534.4 .B44 2002
268'.67--dc21
                                                  2002001630

10 9 8 7 6 5 4 3 2 1          11 10 09 08 07 06 05 04 03 02

Printed in the United States of America.

# Contents

**Introduction** . . . . . . . . . . . . . . . . . . . . . . . . . . . . . . . . . . . . . . . . . . . . . . . . .7

**Back-Seat Driver** . . . . . . . . . . . . . . . . . . . . . . . . . . . . . . . . . . . .11
*God's Sovereignty, Submitting to Others*

**Captain Stupendous** . . . . . . . . . . . . . . . . . . . . . . . . . . . . . . .15
*New Life, Christlikeness*

**Clean Break** . . . . . . . . . . . . . . . . . . . . . . . . . . . . . . . . . . . . . . . .19
*Devotion to Christ, Sin*

**Crocodile Wannabe** . . . . . . . . . . . . . . . . . . . . . . . . . . . . . . . . .23
*Media Influence, Responsibility*

**Dodge Ball** . . . . . . . . . . . . . . . . . . . . . . . . . . . . . . . . . . . . . . . . .27
*Violence, Forgiveness*

**Dog's Best Friend** . . . . . . . . . . . . . . . . . . . . . . . . . . . . . . . . . .30
*God's Love, Thanksgiving*

**Easter: The Sequel** . . . . . . . . . . . . . . . . . . . . . . . . . . . . . . . . .34
*Salvation, The Relevance of the Bible*

**Go With the Flow!** . . . . . . . . . . . . . . . . . . . . . . . . . . . . . . . . . .39
*Peer Pressure, Integrity*

**Gray Matter** . . . . . . . . . . . . . . . . . . . . . . . . . . . . . . . . . . . . . . . .44
*Absolute Truth, Sharing Your Faith*

**The Injustice League** . . . . . . . . . . . . . . . . . . . . . . . . . . . . . . .49
*Racism and Prejudice, Judging*

**It's Malachi!** . . . . . . . . . . . . . . . . . . . . . . . . . . . . . . . . . . . . . . . .53
Bible Study, Heaven

**Just Listen** . . . . . . . . . . . . . . . . . . . . . . . . . . . . . . . . . . . . . . .57
Hearing God, Impure Motives

**Loose Lips** . . . . . . . . . . . . . . . . . . . . . . . . . . . . . . . . . . . . . . . .60
Gossip, Trust

**One More Thing** . . . . . . . . . . . . . . . . . . . . . . . . . . . . . . . . . . .64
Facing Temptation, Premarital Sex

**One Willing Monk** . . . . . . . . . . . . . . . . . . . . . . . . . . . . . . . . . .68
Sacrifice, Following God's Will

**The Reason** . . . . . . . . . . . . . . . . . . . . . . . . . . . . . . . . . . . . . . .73
Christmas, The Urgency of Following Christ

**Samson 3000** . . . . . . . . . . . . . . . . . . . . . . . . . . . . . . . . . . . . . .77
Focus, Talents

**The Switch** . . . . . . . . . . . . . . . . . . . . . . . . . . . . . . . . . . . . . . . .81
Obeying Parents, Stereotypes

**The Talking Mime** . . . . . . . . . . . . . . . . . . . . . . . . . . . . . . . . .85
Hypocrisy, Persecution

**Use Your Legs** . . . . . . . . . . . . . . . . . . . . . . . . . . . . . . . . . . . . .89
Relying on God, Pride

**Topical Index** . . . . . . . . . . . . . . . . . . . . . . . . . . . . . . . . . . . . .93

**Scripture Index** . . . . . . . . . . . . . . . . . . . . . . . . . . . . . . . . . . . .94

**It's Malachi!** . . . . . . . . . . . . . . . . . . . . . . . . . . . . . . . . . . . . . . . . .53
*Bible Study, Heaven*

**Just Listen** . . . . . . . . . . . . . . . . . . . . . . . . . . . . . . . . . . . . . . . . . . .57
*Hearing God, Impure Motives*

**Loose Lips** . . . . . . . . . . . . . . . . . . . . . . . . . . . . . . . . . . . . . . . . . . .60
*Gossip, Trust*

**One More Thing** . . . . . . . . . . . . . . . . . . . . . . . . . . . . . . . . . . . . . . .64
*Facing Temptation, Premarital Sex*

**One Willing Monk** . . . . . . . . . . . . . . . . . . . . . . . . . . . . . . . . . . . . .68
*Sacrifice, Following God's Will*

**The Reason** . . . . . . . . . . . . . . . . . . . . . . . . . . . . . . . . . . . . . . . . . . .73
*Christmas, The Urgency of Following Christ*

**Samson 3000** . . . . . . . . . . . . . . . . . . . . . . . . . . . . . . . . . . . . . . . . .77
*Focus, Talents*

**The Switch** . . . . . . . . . . . . . . . . . . . . . . . . . . . . . . . . . . . . . . . . . . .81
*Obeying Parents, Stereotypes*

**The Talking Mime** . . . . . . . . . . . . . . . . . . . . . . . . . . . . . . . . . . . . .85
*Hypocrisy, Persecution*

**Use Your Legs** . . . . . . . . . . . . . . . . . . . . . . . . . . . . . . . . . . . . . . . .89
*Relying on God, Pride*

**Topical Index** . . . . . . . . . . . . . . . . . . . . . . . . . . . . . . . . . . . . . . . . .93

**Scripture Index** . . . . . . . . . . . . . . . . . . . . . . . . . . . . . . . . . . . . . . .94

# Contents

**Introduction** . . . . . . . . . . . . . . . . . . . . . . . . . . . . . . . . . . . . . . . . . .7

**Back-Seat Driver** . . . . . . . . . . . . . . . . . . . . . . . . . . . . . . . . .11
    *God's Sovereignty, Submitting to Others*

**Captain Stupendous** . . . . . . . . . . . . . . . . . . . . . . . . . . . .15
    *New Life, Christlikeness*

**Clean Break** . . . . . . . . . . . . . . . . . . . . . . . . . . . . . . . . . . . .19
    *Devotion to Christ, Sin*

**Crocodile Wannabe** . . . . . . . . . . . . . . . . . . . . . . . . . . . . .23
    *Media Influence, Responsibility*

**Dodge Ball** . . . . . . . . . . . . . . . . . . . . . . . . . . . . . . . . . . . . .27
    *Violence, Forgiveness*

**Dog's Best Friend** . . . . . . . . . . . . . . . . . . . . . . . . . . . . . .30
    *God's Love, Thanksgiving*

**Easter: The Sequel** . . . . . . . . . . . . . . . . . . . . . . . . . . . . .34
    *Salvation, The Relevance of the Bible*

**Go With the Flow!** . . . . . . . . . . . . . . . . . . . . . . . . . . . . . .39
    *Peer Pressure, Integrity*

**Gray Matter** . . . . . . . . . . . . . . . . . . . . . . . . . . . . . . . . . . . .44
    *Absolute Truth, Sharing Your Faith*

**The Injustice League** . . . . . . . . . . . . . . . . . . . . . . . . . . .49
    *Racism and Prejudice, Judging*

# Dedication

*I dedicate this book to Todd Cook at Hoffmantown West for first encouraging me to write skits, to Mosaic for performing them, to Group Workcamps for using them, and to Group Publishing, Inc., for printing them. Most of all, thanks to Jesus for the inspiration and to my bride, Jill, for always listening.*

## Ultimate Skits: 20 Parables for Driving Home Your Point

Copyright © 2002 Bryan Belknap

Visit our Web site: **www.grouppublishing.com**
Visit Mosaic's Web site: **www.mosaic.org**

**Credits**
Author: Bryan Belknap
Editor: Kelli B. Trujillo
Creative Development Editor: Amy Simpson
Chief Creative Officer: Joani Schultz
Copy Editor: Betty Taylor
Art Director: Kari K. Monson
Computer Graphic Artist: Stephen Beer
Illustrator: Matt Wood
Production Manager: Dodie Tipton

**Library of Congress Cataloging-in-Publication Data**
Belknap, Bryan.
   Ultimate skits : 20 parables for driving home your point / Bryan Belknap
        p. cm.
Includes indexes.
   ISBN 0-7644-2354-1 (pbk. : alk. paper)
  1.   Drama in Christian education.   I. Title.
   BV1534.4 .B44 2002
   268'.67--dc21

                                                    2002001630

10 9 8 7 6 5 4 3 2 1        11 10 09 08 07 06 05 04 03 02

Printed in the United States of America.

# Ultimate skits

## 20 Parables for Driving Home Your Point

Bryan Belknap

**Flagship church resources**
*from* Group Publishing

# *Introduction*

## Drama as Parable

Imagine Jesus sitting down and telling a story about seeds, fishing, and vineyards to...twenty-first-century American teenagers. *Huh?* Most of them wouldn't even have a clue what he was talking about!

If Jesus wandered into your local school's cafeteria today, he'd probably use references to extreme sports, TV, fast food, and Web sites to reveal his truth. His parables always used the language of the culture to impart meaning. The dramas in *Ultimate Skits* are based on that same principle—that using the familiar will help people more readily grasp important spiritual truths. That's why you'll find references to pop culture, game shows, and sporting events woven throughout the twenty skits in *Ultimate Skits*.

Jesus' parables were dramatic narratives that imparted life-changing spiritual truth. He rarely explained the meaning of his parables. Instead he wanted to stir up questions in his listeners and prompt them to seek out real answers. By leaving the parables open-ended, people of all ages in completely different life stages could personally receive his message. Biblical teaching touches people in widely different ways while still directing them to God's truth.

Think back to the possibly all-time fave parable of the prodigal son (Luke 15:11-32). How many different but equally powerful messages have you received from this simple story? Have you identified with different characters at different times in your life? Now, think of how narrow this tale would be if Jesus had told his audience exactly what the parable meant. You could get only one sermon and one interpretation from the good Samaritan (Luke 10:25-37) if Jesus had provided commentary on the parable. Jesus' other memorable parables, such as the good shepherd (John 10:1-18), the unmerciful servant (Matthew 18:21-35), or the laborers in the vineyard (Matthew 20:1-6), would lose some of their freshness, nuance, and depth if he had provided a "leader's guide" to explain them.

Using open-ended parable skits in your ministry will allow audience members to experience biblical truth in ways that apply directly to their life situations. Based on their personal experiences and their individual faith walks, audience members can glean a variety of scriptural meanings from each drama—meanings that might be vastly different from one another. That's why these dramas can be used with audiences from middle school to midlife crisis to "Midge, where're my dentures?" The same story will challenge different people in different ways. That's why these stories are perfect for teenagers—teens can work together to perform the sketches and will uncover the spiritual truth for themselves. Knowledge gained through work and experience will last longer than ideas handed to them on a platter.

## Using Drama in Your Ministry

These skits will definitely make an impact, but that's not to say you can perform one of these sketches and sit back while the repentant masses storm the altar. As you use these parables, make sure they don't simply stand alone, but instead tie them closely to the theme of your youth night, Bible study, sermon, or small group. We use drama almost every week at Mosaic, my home church. Mosaic, an innovative congregation in Los Angeles, is recognized as a Flagship church by Group Publishing and we have used several of the dramas in this book in Mosaic's ministry. The dramas we use run the gamut, from hilarious to deathly serious, from monologue to experimental. Every one relates directly to the sermon, but gives the congregation some flesh to attach to Pastor Erwin McManus' words.

By incorporating the parable into the theme of your event, yet leaving the meaning of the drama open to interpretation, you can step in and pull on the spiritual hook that will influence your audience most, explaining as much or as little as needed to convey the point. Using discussion to debrief the dramas is another great option for helping audience members get the most out of the parable.

Sure, I had a primary illustration in mind when I wrote each drama, but why limit your ministry to my perspective? Tailor this book to the needs of your ministry. That's why I've included *two* sets of discussion questions and topics for each parable—so you can use either of these suggestions or take a different direction.

## Postmodern Parable Performance Tips

This is a book of dramas, so obviously people act them out in front of an audience. (We're not reinventing the wheel here, just adding some sweet rims.) The following tips may help make the dramas more memorable:

**Directing:** The best thing you can do is let your actors do what comes naturally. Let them change their lines if they can't get them down or switch their blocking if it trips them up. Anything that forces the actor to concentrate on *doing* something instead of simply *being* the character hurts performance. Your job is to make the actors as comfortable as possible so they can focus on creating a believable performance.

**Cast:** First, enlist people who are willing. God will use an eager and teachable heart every time. Encourage your cast to practice often and pray for rehearsals and the performance. Don't be locked down by the age or gender called for in the script. If you don't have enough guys for a skit, make some of the roles female. Most of the dialogue is gender- and age-neutral, so mold the situations to fit the actors you have available. The same goes for ages. Although teenagers can easily play adults (heck, adults play teens all the time on TV), you might want to change a character's age. For example, if you felt it would help your audience better connect with the characters, you could make Bud and Rod ("Use Your Legs," p. 89) teenagers working on their summer job. Do whatever it takes to draw the audience into the story.

**Setting:** Try to get furniture whenever you can. A couch and side table will cover more of the set than a single chair, which will leave it looking bare. Make sure to angle all of your furniture toward the audience. Sure, the actors won't be looking directly at one another, but they already know what's going to happen. The audience *must* hear clearly what the actors say for the parable to take hold. Remind your actors *never* to turn their backs to the audience (unless they're looking to catch a tomato in the back).

**Props:** Props for skits of this type usually fall in the "It's better to ask forgiveness than permission" category. Most of the props you'll need sit somewhere in your church building; they just need to be "borrowed" for a couple hours! If you can't find a prop on-site, ask your actors to hunt it down. (They want their parable to look as good as possible.) If the usual suspects turn up dry, you can seek rentals, donations, and even hit up the high school or college drama department. The stuff's out there; you just gotta find it.

**Media:** These optional suggestions are five-cent tricks that will add ten bucks of quality to your drama! Setting up a screen in the background of your stage and using quick video clips, PowerPoint slides, or playing audio sound effects will not only enhance your performance, but also transport your audience directly to the scene. For example, simply show the exterior of a house to set up "The Switch" (p. 81) or show footage of cars racing before "Back-Seat Driver" (p. 11). Whenever possible, throw in sound effects, such as audience applause, theme songs, and slaps or hits. Even if the timing is off, sound effects add serious spice to an already tasty entree.

If you choose to use footage in a skit from a copyrighted video, your church can obtain an umbrella license from the Motion Picture Licensing Corporation. Just visit www.mplc.com or call (800) 462-8855 for more information.

**Discussion Questions:** Select which theme you'd like to focus on, and use the four to six suggested discussion questions to help audience members unpack the meaning of the parable and apply it to their personal lives.

# A Word About Creativity

*Remember*—these parables are road maps, not sacred text. Mold, morph, tweak, and twist these skits to meet the needs of your audience and your ministry. Let the actors' personalities and humor shine through. These dashes of inspiration create unforgettable teaching moments for your ministry.

Dramas also help people connect more deeply with their Creator. One of Mosaic's core values is, "Creativity is the natural result of spirituality." God is the source of all inspiration and originality. I pray these postmodern parables will become a source of spiritual growth for both the audience and the actors in your ministry.

# Back-Seat Driver

## Themes

- God's Sovereignty (1 Chronicles 29:11-13)
- Submitting to Others (Hebrews 13:17)

## The Cast

**Max:** Professional race car driver, wearing a jumpsuit, microphone headset, and a helmet that does not cover his mouth

**Eugene:** Know-it-all fan

## The Setting:

Inside a stock car. To create this scene, place two plush, high-backed chairs side by side at center stage. Hang a sheet over the backs of the chairs. Lean a tire against each chair to make it look more like a car, and have Max hold the steering wheel in his hands.

## Props and Costumes:

A flash camera, a steering wheel, two plush high-backed chairs, a sheet, two tires, a microphone headset, a jumpsuit that resembles a race car driver's outfit, a helmet

## Media Option:

Use video footage of racing stock cars and sound effects of cars racing.

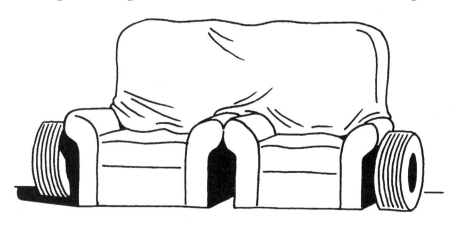

*Max is seated in the driver's-side chair, holding the steering wheel and pretending to drive. Eugene is hiding behind the two chairs, in the "back seat" of the car, with the camera.*

*Option: Play the footage of racing cars to introduce the scene, and let the sound of racing cars run through the entire piece.*

*The scene begins as Max talks into his headset, concentrating hard as he drives his car.*

**Max:** The car's dragging a little. *(Pause.)* Copy that.

*(Quietly, Eugene peeks his head out from the back seat.)*

**Max:** What? I see him.

*(Eugene ducks back behind the seat again. Max downshifts and makes some maneuvers before settling down again.)*

**Max:** That'll keep him off until the next lap.

*(Eugene again peeks over the back seat and slowly raises a camera to his face. He takes a picture, with the flash going off brightly.)*

**Max:** What on earth! *(Max glances back and sees Eugene.)* Who are you?

**Eugene:** Eugene Preston! *(He holds out his hand to shake, but Max doesn't take it.)* Right. Keep 'em at ten and two.

**Max:** *(Into headset)* Charlie! I've got someone in my car!

**Eugene:** I'm nobody. Just pretend I'm not even here.

**Max:** I've got to pit now! *(Listens.)* Fine! *(Max focuses on the road and is furious.)*

**Eugene:** Can I stay?

**Max:** If I pit now I'll lose.

**Eugene:** We can take 'em, Max. Stay on the inside, and hold your ground.

**Max:** *We?* Whaddya mean *we?* I'm driving here.

**Eugene:** Of course! I mean, you're the pro here.

**Max:** That's right, so sit back and can it.

**Eugene:** Whatever you say, you're the boss. *(Long pause.)* I've just got one teeny, tiny suggestion.

**Max:** How many races have you driven in?

**Eugene:** I watch them every weekend, religiously. I never miss.

**Max:** *(Supremely annoyed)* How many races have you actually driven a real car in?

**Eugene:** *(Sheepishly)* None.

**Max:** I've won two national championships, so let me do the driving.

**Eugene:** You're right. You're absolutely right. I'm sorry. I'll just get out of your hair and let you do your job. I'll watch and learn from the master. You won't even know I'm here.

*(Eugene again hides behind the seat. Max concentrates on the road.)*

**Eugene:** Wings.

**Max:** What?!

*(Eugene's head pops back into view.)*

**Eugene:** It's perfect! If you use jet airplane wings, you not only get better lift and handling but it's impossible for other cars to pass.

**Max:** The more you talk, the more proof I have that you're a complete imbecile.

**Eugene:** *(Pouting)* It's only an idea.

**Max:** Keep 'em to yourself.

*(Silence.)*

**Eugene:** Can I drive?

**Max:** No!

**Eugene:** Just let me touch the steering wheel.

*(Eugene reaches over the seat to touch the steering wheel, and Max slaps away his hand.)*

**Max:** Are you completely deranged! I'm driving!

**Eugene:** What's the big deal? Let me drive for a few seconds—maybe even take a turn.

**Max:** We're not cruising slow in the driveway, here. I'm going 180 miles per hour!

**Eugene:** I've gone 210 miles per hour in Gran Turismo.

**Max:** That's it.

*(Max slams on the brakes, sending Eugene flying into the front seat with him.)*

**Eugene:** You stopped!

**Max:** Get out.

**Eugene:** But you're going to lose!

**Max:** I'm not winning and giving you delusions about your abilities. Get out!

**Eugene:** But I'm your biggest fan!

**Max:** Now!

*(Eugene climbs out of the car, turns, and pokes his head back through the window.)*

**Eugene:** Can I get an autograph?

# Discussion Questions—God's Sovereignty

- Have you ever had a "back-seat driver"—someone telling you what to do even though you already knew? How did it make you feel?

- If you think of your life as a race car, who's sitting in the driver's seat?

- Read aloud 1 Chronicles 29:11-13. Why do we sometimes take the "controls" of our life from God when he's all-knowing and all-powerful?

- What usually happens when you take control of your life instead of letting God run the show?

- In what ways can you increase your belief that God's in control of things?

- This week, how can you learn to rely more completely on God?

# Discussion Questions—Submitting to Others

- Why didn't Eugene just sit back quietly and let Max drive?

- Who has God placed in the driver's seat in your life?

- Read aloud Hebrews 13:17. What does the word *submit* mean to you?

- What are the benefits of willingly submitting to someone?

- What blessings will come from being obedient?

# Captain Stupendous

## Themes

- New Life (Acts 9:10-27)
- Christlikeness (Ephesians 5:1-6)

## The Cast

**Jen:** Young woman with a purse

**Captain Stupendous:** Superhero, wearing a traditional superhero costume

**Mugger:** Thug

## The Setting:

An alley. To create this scene, place a metal trash can to one side and spread trash across the floor.

## Props and Costumes:

A cap gun (or prop gun with a gunshot sound effect), a purse, a superhero costume (for example, tights, a cape, and a mask), a trash can, trash

## Media Option:

Use a fist-punch sound effect and a PowerPoint slide that reads, "A deserted alley downtown."

*The Mugger crouches behind the garbage can with the cap gun. Jen and Captain Stupendous are offstage.*

*Option: Show the PowerPoint slide to introduce the scene.*

*The scene begins as Jen walks into the alley. Suddenly the Mugger, armed with a pistol, jumps from behind the garbage can and stops her.*

**Mugger:** Give me your purse.

**Jen:** Help!!!

**Mugger:** Can it! No one can hear you.

*(Captain Stupendous runs in from offstage and leaps between Jen and the Mugger.)*

**Captain:** Justice always hears a cry for help.

**Jen:** Captain Stupendous!

**Mugger:** More like Captain Stupid.

*(The Mugger shoots his gun, but the bullets merely bounce off Captain Stupendous' chest. Captain Stupendous steps forward and punches the Mugger, who falls to the floor unconscious. [Option: Play the fist-punch sound effect.] The Mugger should remain on the floor throughout the rest of the drama.)*

**Jen:** You saved my life!

**Captain:** I'm only purging the street of wickedness and protecting the defenseless.

**Jen:** Thank you so much. I thought he was going to…Hey, don't I know you?

**Captain:** I don't believe I've had the pleasure of saving your life before, ma'am.

*(Jen tries to look behind the Captain's mask, but he moves his head around, avoiding her gaze.)*

**Jen:** Let me get a good look at you.

**Captain:** You might be thinking of Stupendous Man. People get us confused a lot.

**Jen:** I'm a speech therapist, and I never forget a voice.

**Captain:** *(In a ridiculous fake accent, turning to leave)* I think I hear a defenseless child crying for help. I really must go!

**Jen:** Nick Gillespie! You're Nick Gillespie!

**Captain:** I don't know what you're talking about.

**Jen:** Cut it out, Nick. We graduated together, remember? I'm Jen Holland. You asked me to homecoming sophomore year.

*(The Captain's shoulders slump in defeat.)*

**Captain:** I know who you are, Jen. How are ya doing?

**Jen:** I knew it! It's really you!

**Captain:** Shh! Keep it down! I'm supposed to have a secret identity.

**Jen:** Oh, I won't tell. Don't worry. Wait! Are you going to erase my memory of meeting you?

**Captain:** Naw, I don't have that power.

**Jen:** Look at you, a big time superhero! I read about your exploits all the time in the paper, but never would've guessed it was you.

**Captain:** I stay busy.

**Jen:** How'd you get the superpowers?

**Captain:** I was hiking and found this cave filled with nuclear waste. The radiation got in my bones and changed me forever. Now I can fly, stop bullets with my chest, X-ray vision, the works.

**Jen:** That is really great. You know, I graduated from Tech. I'm working for the school system now, helping kids and stuff. I mean, it's fun for now, but I'm still writing songs on the side—dreaming about that record deal, just like high school.

**Captain:** I remember. You were always winning the talent shows.

**Jen:** Those were the glory days. *(Pause.)* I can't believe it! Nick Gillespie! You remember your nickname?

**Captain:** I'd rather not.

**Jen:** Naughty Nick, the Ladies Pick! You partied so hard! Weren't you voted "Most Likely to Die a Diseased Wino"?

**Captain:** People change, Jen. I did crazy stuff in high school, but I'm different now. I've got a new life.

**Jen:** We didn't think you'd live past college. You were such a booze hound.

**Captain:** Lucky for you I did.

**Jen:** *(Snaps out of her memories.)* You're right. I'm sorry, I'm just so amazed to see you here, and a superhero! I can't wait to tell Sherry. She'll flip!

**Captain:** My identity's a *secret*, Jen.

**Jen:** Oh, sure, sure. *(She mimes locking her lips with a key and throwing it away.)* Not a soul. *(She shakes the Captain's hand.)* It's so great to see you, and thanks for saving my life.

**Captain:** That's what I do now. Sorry I can't stay and chat, but it's a dangerous city. Lots of people to help.

**Jen:** Right. Oh, hey! Ya know, you could call me for a date if you want. I'd probably say yes this time since you saved my life and all.

**Captain:** Riiiiight. Be careful, Jen. *(Captain Stupendous takes off.)*

**Jen:** I will, Nick. I mean…Captain Stupendous. Thanks. See you at the reunion!

# Discussion Questions—New Life

- Do you know anyone who has dramatically changed his or her life? If so, how?

- Do you think people can change? Why or why not?

- Read aloud Acts 9:10-27. Why were the disciples so afraid of Paul?

- How should someone change when that person comes to know Jesus Christ?

- Do you think people see a change in your life because of Jesus? Why or why not?

- This week, how can you more dramatically display your new life in Christ?

## Discussion Questions—Christlikeness

- If Jen had never seen Nick again after high school, how would she have always remembered him?

- How would your peers remember you if you graduated today and never saw them again?

- Read aloud Ephesians 5:1-6. Why is it so important to be "imitators of God"?

- How can a sinful human being become an imitator of Christlikeness?

- How does living a thankful lifestyle display Jesus to others?

- Do you need to make changes in your lifestyle to better reflect Christ? If so, how will you do that?

# Clean Break

## Themes

- Devotion to Christ (Jeremiah 2:11-13)
- Sin (Romans 6:1-2)

## The Cast

**Nicole:** Teenage girl
**James:** Teenage boy

## The Setting:

A park bench. To create this scene, set a bench (or a pew) in the center of the stage.

## Props and Costumes:

A bench or church pew, regular clothes

*Nicole sits on the bench. The scene begins as James enters from offstage, gives Nicole a quick kiss on the cheek, and sits down.*

**James:** Hey, Nicole. I came as soon as I could. Is everything OK?

**Nicole:** We need to talk.

**James:** Oh no.

**Nicole:** What?

**James:** We always talk when we hang out, so if you say, "We need to talk," it's got to be bad news. I didn't miss an anniversary, did I?

**Nicole:** No.

**James:** Are you OK?

**Nicole:** Me? Oh, yeah. Great. I'm loving life! *(Pause.)* Things are terrible. I don't want to do this.

**James:** It's me, James, your boyfriend. I love you! If you can't tell me, who are you going to tell?

**Nicole:** I want to break up.

**James:** Don't tell me that.

**Nicole:** I didn't want this to happen.

**James:** Then we'll forget you said anything. I'll call you tonight. Later!

*(James stands to leave, but Nicole grabs his arm.)*

**Nicole:** No, James. We can't just forget it.

**James:** This is about that karate flick I went to with the team on Friday.

**Nicole:** No.

**James:** You're still sore I missed your recital? That was a year ago! I've been to every one since.

**Nicole:** No, I…

**James:** *(Interrupts.)* Is it Valentine's Day in France?

**Nicole:** Would you stop! You haven't done anything wrong! You are the nicest, most kind, loving, and considerate guy I've ever met.

**James:** *(Smiles.)* Thanks, honey. *(Frowns.)* But you want to break up?

**Nicole:** Yes.

**James:** *(Sits beside her.)* I don't understand.

**Nicole:** We've been going out for a year and a half…

**James:** One year, seven months, and three days, to be exact.

**Nicole:** Anyway, I think it's time we move on.

**James:** Move on to what?

**Nicole:** I don't know—greener pastures.

**James:** It sounds like we're retiring.

**Nicole:** There's a whole world out there! Tons of new and exciting things we need to experience. You like *Star Trek*, right? That whole "boldly going" thing.

**James:** Let's experience boldly going together.

**Nicole:** I don't want to be tied down! I need to be free and see what's out there.

**James:** But you said I'm the coolest guy you've ever met.

**Nicole:** I know…but I can't find a cooler guy if I'm with you.

**James:** That guy may not exist.

**Nicole:** I know, but I'm bored. There's so much I haven't done yet.

**James:** You don't have to experience everything. Some things are better left alone.

**Nicole:** I don't care.

**James:** So basically you're telling me you love the relationship we've been building, but you want to see what else is out there.

**Nicole:** Exactly! I mean, maybe I won't find anything and we'll get back together.

**James:** It might be too late.

**Nicole:** I guess I'll have to take that chance.

**James:** Are you sure?

**Nicole:** We can still be friends.

**James:** No, I'm an all-or-nothing kind of guy.

**Nicole:** I'm sorry. This is for the best.

**James:** For who?

*(Silence.)*

**James:** Give me a call if you change your mind. Goodbye, Nicole.

**Nicole:** Goodbye, James.

*(James and Nicole exit on opposite sides of the stage.)*

# Discussion Questions—Devotion to Christ

- Have you ever been "replaced" by someone else, either in dating, friendship, sports, or something else? How did it make you feel?

- Read aloud Jeremiah 2:11-13. What reasons do people have for replacing Jesus in their lives?

- How do you think God feels when someone "breaks up" with him?

- Do you protect your relationship with Jesus as you would a dating relationship? Why or why not?

- Does anything threaten to replace Jesus in your life right now? How can you guard that relationship?

# Discussion Questions—Sin

- What is one sin you are curious about trying?

- What are the possible consequences of participating in that sin?

- Why do people often want to try things even though they know those things will probably cause pain in the end?

- Read aloud Romans 6:1-2. If God forgives our sin, why shouldn't we try everything once?

- In your opinion, do you have to experience sin to appreciate grace? Why or why not?

- How can you resist acting on your curiosity about sin?

# Crocodile Wannabe

## Themes

- Media Influence (2 Corinthians 10:3-5)
- Responsibility (Ezekiel 18:20-22)

## The Cast

**Tamara:** Bubbly, cheesy, and clueless talk show host, wearing professional clothes

**Billy:** Regular teenage guy, covered in bandages, wearing a sling, and using a crutch

**Audience:** For added humor, have someone hold up cue cards to prompt audience reactions. For example, cards could say, "Applause," "Awwww," and "Ooooo."

## The Setting:

A talk show. To create this scene, place two stuffed chairs in the center of the stage. Angle the chairs toward each other and the audience. Between the chairs, place a small coffee table, with coffee mugs and a vase of flowers.

## Props and Costumes:

A crutch, a sling, bandages, audience cue cards, two chairs, a small coffee table, coffee mugs, a vase of flowers, a woman's professional outfit (such as a pantsuit).

## Media Option:

Use a theme song sound effect and a PowerPoint slide that reads, "Tamara Talk."

*Tamara is seated in one of the plush chairs, and Billy is offstage.*

*Option: Show the PowerPoint slide for Tamara Talk, and play the theme music to introduce the scene. Fade the music during Tamara's introduction.*

*The scene begins as Tamara stands up, facing the audience with the chairs behind her.*

**Tamara:** Welcome to *Tamara Talk*. I'm Tamara, and we're going to spend the next half-hour sitting around talking.

*(Audience applauds.)*

**Tamara:** You people are too much! Thank you. My special guest today is a brave little boy with an incredible story. Please welcome Billy Preston!

*(The audience and Tamara clap for Billy as he hobbles onstage. Tamara crosses to him and helps him sit in a chair. She sits across from him.)*

**Tamara:** Now, Billy. I understand that you survived a vicious crocodile attack.

**Billy:** Yes, ma'am.

**Tamara:** We're just talking here on *Tamara Talk*, so call me Tamara.

**Billy:** OK, Tamara.

**Tamara:** When did this happen?

**Billy:** A week and a half ago.

**Tamara:** And how long will it take you to recover?

**Billy:** Six months.

*(The audience and Tamara groan with sympathy.)*

**Tamara:** That's awful!

**Billy:** I'm missing track season and summer camp, and there's only reruns on TV!

**Tamara:** You poor, poor dear. Can you tell us what happened?

**Billy:** I was at the zoo…

**Tamara:** *(Interrupts.)* I just love the monkeys. Aren't they the cutest! I had one spit on me once—just precious!

*(The audience applauds their approval.)*

**Tamara:** Go on, Billy.

**Billy:** We were watching the crocodiles and alligators and stuff, and I decided to wrestle one.

**Tamara:** What on earth would inspire you to do something so dangerous?

**Billy:** Jaws Sherwin does it all the time. He's the Alligator Stalker on Animal Channel. He's always grabbing dangerous reptiles on his show and wrestling them to the ground.

**Tamara:** And you thought you could do it, too?

**Billy:** Sure! He makes it look so easy, and I wanted to be just like him.

**Tamara:** *(To audience)* We all have our heroes, don't we? When I was a girl, I wanted to be that spunky little gymnast Mary Lou Retton so bad. I spent all day practicing in the back yard until I broke my wrists doing back handsprings. I learned to write with my feet because of that. It's true—

either one—I can write with my feet! *(To Billy)* Tell me, Billy. How did you imitate your hero?

**Billy:** I had to climb a fence and make it through the barbed wire at the top. I covered it with my cousin's coat so I wouldn't get cut. Boy was Aunt Jan mad!

**Tamara:** *(To audience)* I wore this new coat one time that rubbed off red on my blouse. It ruined it! I went home and listened to Ricky Martin all night until I felt better.

**Billy:** What are you talking about?

*(Long pause and silence.)*

**Tamara:** Do you have any brothers or sisters?

**Billy:** Yeah. *(To "viewers")* Hey, Stan! Hi, Julie!

*(The audience and Tamara respond with "Awwwws.")*

**Tamara:** That was so sweet. Wasn't that sweet? So you got in the cage. Where were the security guards?

**Billy:** We distracted them by setting the lemur's tail on fire.

**Tamara:** *(To audience)* All of you kids watching at home, don't play with fire. It's bad, very bad! *(To Billy)* Go ahead, sweetie.

**Billy:** I saw this really old croc, and figured he wouldn't put up much of a fight, so I jumped on him just like Jaws Sherwin does.

**Tamara:** That's when you got bit?

**Billy:** The first time. He got my arm. I ran away as quick as I could.

*(The audience "Oooos" in pain.)*

**Tamara:** You poor thing.

**Billy:** My arm was pretty messed up, so I went for one of the babies with my good arm.

**Tamara:** Persistence will get you everywhere in life, honey. *(To audience)* This boy is going to go far, isn't he?

*(The audience applauds.)*

**Billy:** I got a good grip on him and took him to the edge to show my cousin. That's when the big one, musta been the mama, caught me from behind.

*(Tamara covers her eyes, and the audience hisses in pain.)*

**Billy:** Luckily, security got there and hauled me out.

**Tamara:** And that's when they gave you a ticket for trespassing. How awful.

**Billy:** It's not my fault! I blame Alligator Stalker. I mean, I never would've thought of wrestling a crocodile if I hadn't seen it on his show. Ya know, in real life, kids don't think. We think we're invincible, so we don't worry about what will happen.

**Tamara:** Isn't that the truth? Let's hear it for Billy Preston, a very brave victim. Here's a young man who watched TV to learn and ended up being manipulated.

*(Audience applause.)*

**Tamara:** It's time to hold this Alligator Stalker responsible for leading impressionable youth astray.

*(Wild applause.)*

**Tamara:** We'll be back after this break to talk more about how TV exploits our youth when we meet Cindy, a precious little girl in a body cast because she tried to fly like the Powerpuff Girls. You're talking with Tamara on *Tamara Talk*.

# Discussion Questions—Media Influence

- What stories have you heard about people imitating what they see in the media?

- How does the media influence people's lives?

- Read aloud 2 Corinthians 10:3-5. According to this Scripture, how can Christians deal with media messages?

- How can you discern the "knowledge of God" and "take captive every thought"?

- How will evaluating media messages through the filter of the gospel help increase your faith? How will it help you relate to non-Christians?

# Discussion Questions—Responsibility

- What examples of crazy stunts have you heard of people pulling and then blaming someone else for?

- Why is it so hard for people to take responsibility for their actions?

- Read aloud Ezekiel 18:20-22. What does verse 20 mean to you?

- What reasons do people have for passing blame for their actions onto someone else?

- What happens when you pass responsibility for your actions onto someone or something else?

- Does God's forgiveness make it easier for you to accept responsibility for your failures? Why or why not?

# Dodge Ball

## Themes

- Violence (Genesis 4:3-8)
- Forgiveness (Matthew 18:21-35)

## The Cast

**Zane:** Teenage boy, wearing gym clothes

**Jackson:** Teenage boy, wearing gym clothes

**Joyner:** Someone offstage who periodically throws the ball

## The Setting:

A Dodge Ball game. The actors should stand in front of a wall that Joyner can throw the ball against.

## Props and Costumes:

A red rubber dodge ball, gym clothes

*Zane and Jackson are standing against a wall. The scene begins as Zane and Jackson dance back and forth against the wall and a red dodge ball flies at them and misses, bouncing off the wall. The ball is thrown at them periodically throughout the drama, missing every time until the end.*

**Zane:** I hate this game.

**Jackson:** Aren't we too old for this?

**Zane:** *(Sarcastically)* They think it helps us get all our "aggressions" out.

**Jackson:** Like getting pegged by a ball makes me feel better.

*(Both guys flinch and moan as they react to someone offstage getting pegged.)*

**Zane:** Ouch! Right in the face.

**Jackson:** That'll leave a mark. *(Yells out)* Hey, Calvin! Instant replay! (*Jackson acts out in humorously overexaggerated slow motion the shock, fear, and impact of getting hit in the face.*)

*(Another ball comes close to hitting the boys.)*

**Jackson:** Whoa! Watch it, Joyner!

**Zane:** Someone's been eating Wheaties!

**Jackson:** Hey man, did I tell you? I got a new high score in Death Sport.

**Zane:** How?

**Jackson:** I'll show ya. You can disembowel people with this secret move for major bonus points.

*(The dodge ball hits the wall.)*

**Zane:** Didja see *Vengeance Force* last night?

**Jackson:** Naw. Had to finish a report. What happened?

**Zane:** Striker had special ops totally destroy the vigilantes—we're talking tanks and flamethrowers and kung fu and everything!

*(The dodge ball hits the wall.)*

**Jackson:** Can you believe what Phil did to me?

**Zane:** What?

**Jackson:** The jerk told Michelle that I have congenital jock itch.

**Zane:** You do.

**Jackson:** I know that! He didn't have to tell Michelle, though. I'm gonna kill him.

**Zane:** You gotta let it go.

**Jackson:** I know. It'd be fun to get him back somehow, though.

**Zane:** Like how?

**Jackson:** I dunno. Maybe something involving dripping acid and fire ants.

**Zane:** And make him watch *Oprah* while doing it.

**Jackson:** That's some serious torture, man. You're heartless.

*(The dodge ball hits the wall.)*

**Jackson:** I'm just messin'. Phil's a cool guy when he's not bein' a tool. Didja hear about Josh?

**Zane:** What an idiot.

**Jackson:** He had to spend the night in jail and everything.

**Zane:** What was he thinking?

**Jackson:** No clue. Everybody knows violence doesn't help. *(Jackson gets hit with the ball while he and Zane aren't paying attention. He yells)* I can't believe you hit me! You're a dead man, Joyner!

## Discussion Questions—Violence

- What were the sources of violence in the drama?

- Why do you think violence is so common in society today?

- Read aloud Genesis 4:3-8. How many of today's reasons for violence were around during Cain and Abel's time?

- What does this reveal about the nature of violence? Explain.

- What are some constructive ways for people to deal with their rage?

- How can you help friends deal with their violent feelings?

## Discussion Questions—Forgiveness

- Have you ever wanted to get back at someone? What happened?

- Does revenge make you feel better? Why or why not?

- Read aloud Matthew 18:21-35. What makes it so hard to forgive people who've wronged you?

- Why is forgiveness always better than revenge?

- What has God forgiven you for in your life?

- Do you need to forgive anyone this week? How can you do that?

# Dog's Best Friend

## Themes

- God's Love (Romans 5:6-9)
- Thanksgiving (Psalm 107:8-9)

## The Cast

**Rob:** Teenage guy

**Snoop:** Dog, preferably real and well-trained, but a stuffed animal is also OK. Someone offstage will be Snoop's voice.

## The Setting:

A back yard. To create this scene, place a doghouse on one side of the stage and a bush or plant at the rear of the stage.

## Props:

A doghouse, a bush, a dog (plush or real), and a microphone

*Rob and a dog are center stage. The actor who speaks as Snoop's voice is offstage with the microphone.*

*The scene begins as Rob plays with his dog in the back yard.*

**Rob:** *(In a baby voice)* I love you, Snoop, yes I do! You're the best dog, yes you are.

**Snoop:** Thank you, Rob.

**Rob:** Ahhh! *(Rob jumps up in fear and confusion. He looks around the yard.)* Who's there? Come on out.

**Snoop:** It's rude to turn your back when someone's talking to you.

*(Rob searches the yard, looking behind the doghouse and the bush.)*

**Rob:** And it's rude to trespass. Is that you, Hank? Where are you?

**Snoop:** Rob, look at me!

*(Rob turns around to look at his dog, disbelief covering his face.)*

**Rob:** Yes?

**Snoop:** I'll prove I can talk.

**Rob:** This I gotta hear. OK, prove it.

**Snoop:** Remember the time your girlfriend cooked that special dinner for your anniversary?

**Rob:** So, what about it?

**Snoop:** You told her it was the best thing you'd ever eaten.

**Rob:** Yeah.

**Snoop:** You only ate one bite and fed the rest to me.

*(Rob looks at Snoop in awe. He sits down on the ground.)*

**Snoop:** And what about the time we went for a walk and you threw a rock that smashed out the Johnson's win…

**Rob:** *(Interrupts.)* OK. OK! I believe you. My dog can talk. I can't believe I'm having a conversation with a dog!

**Snoop:** Hey now, don't be prejudiced.

**Rob:** You can't talk! You're a pet that I feed and bathe and pick up poop after. Besides, your lips aren't even moving.

**Snoop:** Just because my lips don't move doesn't mean I can't talk to you. You hear me, don't you?

**Rob:** How did you learn?

**Snoop:** All dogs know how to talk. We just choose not to.

**Rob:** Why?

**Snoop:** Why should we? This way we get fed, have a place to sleep, get lots of love, take naps anytime, and never work a day of our lives.

**Rob:** *(Thinks.)* That's a pretty sweet deal.

**Snoop:** We think of man as dog's best friend.

**Rob:** So why are you giving yourself away?

**Snoop:** After all this time, I just felt like I had to tell you how much I appreciate everything you do for me.

**Rob:** It's no big deal—I don't mind.

**Snoop:** I know, but you do so much—feed me, bathe me, walk me—you even built the doghouse for me.

**Rob:** Yeah, that was a pain.

**Snoop:** You stuck with it even after you pounded your thumb a few times.

**Rob:** Well, I wanted you to have a house.

**Snoop:** That's what I mean. You could have made me sleep on the ground.

**Rob:** (*Shrugs.*) I love you. It's kind of like my job to take care of you. I'm your master.

**Snoop:** That's it! You don't care if I'm good or bad. You might get disappointed in me, but you're always there to care for me. I've never thanked you, and you still love me. Thank you.

**Rob:** I just want you to be happy.

**Snoop:** The least I can do now is let you know that I love you and thank you for all you've done. I'm going to try to be the perfect dog from now on.

**Rob:** (*Scratching Snoop's head*) I'll still love you, Snoop, no matter what you do.

**Snoop:** I know, but I'm going to try my best.

**Rob:** We better go inside.

**Snoop:** Whatever you say.

(*Rob turns to go offstage but stops and turns around.*)

**Rob:** I'm the only one who knows you can talk, right?

**Snoop:** Yes.

**Rob:** Do you think you could find out if Mom and Dad are buying me a car soon?

# Discussion Questions—God's Love

- How did Rob unconditionally love Snoop?

- If someone in your life has unconditional love for you, how does he or she communicate that to you?

- Read aloud Romans 5:6-9. How does God show us unconditional love?

- Why does God show us so much love, especially when we so often forget to thank or acknowledge him?

- Can you deserve God's love? Why or why not?

- In what ways can you thank God for his unconditional love?

# Discussion Questions—Thanksgiving

- What would you do if your pet started talking to you like Snoop talked to Rob?

- Have you ever done something nice for someone and they didn't thank you? How did that make you feel?

- Why aren't people more thankful?

- Read aloud Psalm 107:8-9. In your life, what things has God done for you?

- Did you thank God for these things? If not, why didn't you?

- How can you more often express your thankfulness to God?

# Easter: The Sequel

## Themes

- Salvation (2 Corinthians 5:14-15)
- The Relevance of the Bible (Psalm 119:129-130)

## The Cast

**Ann:** Marketing executive in business attire

**Tommy:** Marketing executive in business attire

**Sue**: Marketing executive in business attire

**JB:** Marketing executive in business attire

(Optional) **Voice:** A deep, ominous voice from offstage reads the text for the Power-Point movie trailer into a microphone.

## The Setting:

A boardroom. To create this scene, place a table with four chairs in the middle of the stage. Create a chart with a diagonal line that goes up and then plateaus. Place the chart on an easel off to one side.

## Props and Costumes:

An easel and a pad of paper with a chart drawn on it, a table, four chairs, four professional outfits (optional: a microphone)

## Media Option:

Use a PowerPoint presentation for the "movie trailer." The movie trailer should be a black screen with the following text:

*One man*

*Loved*

*Feared*

*Murdered*

*Jesus Christ*

*He's back...*

*And he's mad.*

*"I did not come to bring peace, but a sword" (Matthew 10:34b).*

*Easter never hurt so good.*

(Each line should have its own PowerPoint slide.)

*Ann, Tommy, and Sue sit in chairs around the table and face the audience. JB stands and paces back and forth throughout the drama. All the characters deliver their lines at a rapid-fire pace.*

*The scene begins as JB says his first line.*

**JB:** Where do we stand?

**Ann:** Bad.

**Tommy:** Very bad.

**Sue:** Not good.

**JB:** What's wrong?

**Ann:** We've maxed out Easter.

**JB:** What do you mean by *maxed*?

**Tommy:** It's tapped out.

**Sue:** There's no more room for growth.

**JB:** Impossible.

**Ann:** The figures don't lie, JB.

**Tommy:** *(Pointing to chart)* We've been at a sales plateau for two years and expect a decline in two more.

**JB:** We just need something new to generate more excitement.

**Ann:** There's nothing left! We've saturated the religious crowd with cards, paintings, figurines, and anything else marketing could dream up.

**Tommy:** And we've exhausted everyone else with bunnies, eggs, chickens…

**Sue:** Candy, baskets, dresses…

**Tommy:** Video games, cartoons, costumes…

**Sue:** Even theme parks, school supplies, and fast-food endorsements.

**Ann:** We've also done all the crossover marketing possible. Chocolate crosses…

**Tommy:** Feeding the 5,000 with Easter eggs…

**Sue:** Bugs Bunny and Jesus save Easter.

**Ann:** It's all been done.

**JB:** The stock will plummet when investors hear about this! We've got to think of something fast!

**Tommy:** What about a spokesperson?

**Sue:** Yeah, give the holiday some edge. We've always gone pretty touchy feely with it.

**JB:** All those bunnies and eggs and bonnets! Where's the appeal for the fourteen- to thirty-four-year-old male? I want the kid from Des Moines who loves BMX and DMX to shout "Easter kicks cottontail!" Give me blood, give me kung fu—give me something to work with.

**Tommy:** Dinosaurs!

**Sue:** They lay eggs.

**Ann:** They eat people.

**Tommy:** "Don't Go Extinct This Easter."

**Sue:** "Have a T-Rexic Easter!"

**JB:** Dinosaurs are out.

**Tommy:** Out?

**JB:** Look at the numbers. Dinosaurs are as last-century as POGs.

**Ann:** Is nothing sacred?

**JB:** We're making this too hard. Who's our Easter spokesperson?

**Ann:** The bunny.

**JB:** Before that.

**Tommy:** The guy…you know.

**Sue:** With the hair and the glowing head…

**Tommy:** Jesus.

**Ann:** Right! Kinda creepy—we could play the ghost angle.

**JB:** That's what I'm talking about! What do people really know about this guy?

*(Silence.)*

**JB:** Exactly. There's a lot of unknown territory in there we can use. We need to reposition this mystery man, give him some pizazz for the kids, reintroduce him to the public.

**Tommy:** Everybody's seen the miniseries, JB. They know Jesus.

**JB:** There's got to be a different angle.

**Ann:** How about a sequel?

**JB:** What?

**Ann:** We could make Easter longer.

**JB:** I'm listening.

**Ann:** This guy comes back from the dead, right?

**Sue:** That's what our Easter Magic Kit says.

**Ann:** What did he do?

**Tommy:** He…looked for eggs?

**Ann:** No! Look, if someone killed you and you came back to life, what would you do?

**Sue:** I'd get even.

**JB:** Exactly! We extend the holiday and fill in the gaps. What adventures did he have? Did he get even? Was he a scary ghost like Beetlejuice or sweet like Casper?

**Tommy:** Or both!

**Ann:** A Jekyll and Hyde vibe. I like that.

**JB:** That's it, keep the juices flowing. More Jesus means more greeting cards, T-shirts, trinkets…

**Ann:** Missing adventures.

**Tommy:** New sidekicks.

**Sue:** Action figures.

**Tommy:** Books.

**Sue:** Video games.

**All:** Movies!

*Optional: End by darkening the lights and beginning the PowerPoint movie trailer as a voice reads these lines from offstage:*

One man

Loved

Feared

Murdered

Jesus Christ

He's back…

And he's mad.

"I did not come to bring peace, but a sword" (Matthew 10:34b).

Easter never hurt so good.

## Discussion Questions—Salvation

- What beliefs do people have about Jesus?

- Who do you think Jesus is?

- Read aloud 2 Corinthians 5:14-15. What does this verse say about the purpose of Jesus' death and resurrection?

- Do you believe the Bible's claims about Jesus? Why or why not?

- How can you receive forgiveness for your sins?

- Is there any reason for you not to accept Jesus' forgiveness right now?

## Discussion Questions—The Relevance of the Bible

- What advertisements have you seen that make ordinary items seem exciting?

- Do you ever feel as if the Bible should be "updated" or made more "interesting"? Why or why not?

- Read aloud Psalm 119:129-130. How can the Bible be centuries old and still relevant to your life today?

- In what practical and creative ways can we communicate God's Word with relevance?

# Go With the Flow!

## Themes

- Peer Pressure (1 Corinthians 10:12-13)
- Integrity (Amos 5:10)

## The Cast

**Matt Kojak:** Energetic game show host wearing a suit and a slick hairdo

**Quentin Gage:** Superficial, hot, young actor wearing stylish clothes

**Candy Karpinski:** Superficial, attractive, young actress wearing a red dress and high heels

**Killer:** Person wearing a scary mask and a black robe to hide his or her identity

**Contestant:** Youth group student planted in the audience, dressed normally

**Security Guard:** Someone with muscles wearing a security uniform

**Fan:** Teenage girl who can do great "star struck" screams

**Teenage Boy:** Student who can run and scream

**Teenage Girl:** Student who can run and scream

## The Setting:

A game show. To create this scene, place a podium on the right side of the stage, angled toward the audience, for Matt Kojak to stand behind. Also on the right side of the stage, line up four chairs, angled toward the audience, for the contestants to sit in. Place index cards with the trivia questions written on them on the game show host's podium.

## Props and Costumes:

A podium, four chairs, a fake knife, index cards with the trivia questions written on them, an index card marked with an X, tape, a suit, stylish male clothes, a red dress and high heels, a scary mask, a black robe, a security uniform

## Media Option:

Use theme music and applause sound effects and a PowerPoint slide that reads, "Go With the Flow!"

*All actors are offstage except for the Contestant, who is seated with the other audience members. Killer has the fake knife. The index card with the X is taped under the Contestant's chair in the audience.*

*Option: To introduce the scene, show the* Go With the Flow! *PowerPoint slide and play the theme music and applause. Fade music and applause during Matt's opening introduction.*

*The scene begins as Matt Kojak bounds onto the stage.*

**Matt:** Thank you! Thank you, everyone, and welcome to *Go With the Flow!* the game show where everyone's a winner as long as they agree. I'm your host, Matt Kojak, and today's show is very special because we have several celebrity contestants with us. All of their winnings will go to local charities. So, let's meet the contestants! You'll remember our first guest from the blockbuster movie *Return to Titanic*, the hottest young man alive—give a warm welcome to Quentin Gage!

*(Quentin struts out. Suddenly, the Fan runs out, screaming in delight, and locks herself onto his leg in a death grip. Quentin drags her a few feet until the Security Guard grabs her and drags her away as she screams, "I love you! I love you!")*

**Matt:** Welcome to the show, Quentin. You're looking good today.

**Quentin:** I always look good.

**Matt:** Of course. Let's meet our next guest. She's an international television and movie star, everybody's dream girl, Candy Karpinski!

*(Candy walks on stage, blowing kisses and waving.)*

**Matt:** What charity are you giving your winnings to?

**Candy:** Women are not treated with respect today, so I want to help combat that by giving money to a shelter for battered women.

*(Matt and Quentin merely stare at her, obviously checking her out, not hearing a word she says.)*

**Candy:** Matt? Are you listening to me?

**Matt:** Huh? Oh, right. Great! Don't you think, Quentin?

**Quentin:** *(Still staring)* Whatever, man.

*(Candy crosses her arms and rolls her eyes in disgust.)*

**Matt:** Let's meet our third contestant. This film star is known the world over even though you've never seen his face. Please welcome the killer from *Slice & Dice*!

*(The Teenage Boy and Girl run across the stage and into the crowd. They are screaming and followed closely by the Killer, who chases them with a knife. Matt jumps in front of the Killer, blocking his path.)*

**Matt:** Whoa there, fella! Plenty of time for that after the show. Let's win some money for charity, OK?

*(The Killer nods his head yes and joins his fellow contestants.)*

**Matt:** Our final guest, Barney the purple dinosaur, couldn't join us today because we discovered he wasn't famous anymore. So, we need another contestant! Reach under your seat. If you have an index card taped there, you're our lucky fourth contestant!

*(The Contestant finds the card, cheering excitedly.)*

**Matt:** Come on down! You're about to *Go With the Flow!*

*(The Contestant stands next to Matt, jumping up and down with excitement. Matt puts his arm around the Contestant.)*

**Matt:** What's your name, and where are you from?

**Contestant:** *(Gives his or her real name and address.)*

**Matt:** Do you know the rules to *Go With the Flow?*

**Contestant:** No.

**Matt:** It's really simple. I ask a question, and the person who controls the board answers. Then the rest of you say whether you agree or not. If you all go with the flow and agree, you win $500 for charity! How does that sound?

**Contestant:** Great!

**Matt:** Which charity do you want to donate your winnings to?

**Contestant:** *(Gives the name of your church.)*

**Matt:** I'm sure they could put the money to good use there. You get the first question. *(Matt reads from an index card.)* You see someone lying hurt and bleeding on the road. What do you do?

**Contestant:** What is "I would help them"?

**Matt:** Wrong show, but good answer. Quentin?

**Quentin:** Me too, Bob. For sure.

**Matt:** My name is Matt. Candy?

**Candy:** Of course I would help.

**Matt:** Killer?

*(The Killer thinks, shrugs his shoulders, and finally gives the thumbs up sign.)*

**Matt:** Way to go with the flow. You've just won $500 for charity! Here's the next question. Quentin *(reading from an index card),* you're at a huge party with all your friends and several people you want to impress. One of these people offers you some marijuana. What do you do?

**Quentin:** Well, it's a little hard for me to imagine a party where everyone's not trying to impress *me,* but I'm an actor, so I'll try. *(Shuts eyes and imagines.)* I'd have to say I would smoke the joint and definitely inhale.

**Matt:** There's his answer. What do you say, Candy?

**Candy:** I guess so. It's for charity, right?

**Matt:** Whatever you want to believe. Killer?

*(Killer pretends to hold a joint up to his lips and takes a big drag.)*

**Matt:** Looks like everyone's going with the flow. It's up to you.

**Contestant:** No! I wouldn't do that. It's bad for you and it's illegal.

**Matt:** No?! That's going against the flow. I'm sorry, no money for charity on that one. Are you sure you understand the rules?

**Contestant:** Yes, I understand.

**Matt:** All right. Let's continue. Candy *(reading from an index card),* you are offered the lead role in a major motion picture. If you accept the part, though, you'll have to do several steamy love scenes. Will you do it?

**Candy:** I'm assuming it's essential to the plot of the movie.

**Matt:** It always seems to be, doesn't it?

**Candy:** You're right. Sure, I'd do it.

**Matt:** How about you Quent. May I call you Quent?

**Quentin:** No.

**Matt:** Sorry, Quentin.

**Quentin:** I pardon you. What was the question?

**Matt:** Would you do a steamy love scene?

**Quentin:** Sure thing, Pat.

**Matt:** Matt. Killer?

*(Killer starts pulling up his robes to reveal his legs. Matt jumps to stop him.)*

**Matt:** Killer, stop! This is a family show. Well

*(to Contestant),* would you do it?

**Contestant:** No way!

**Matt:** No?! I'm sorry, but that's incorrect. No money awarded.

**Quentin:** How stupid can you be?

**Candy:** Just go with the flow! It's for charity.

**Matt:** OK everyone, I'm sure you can agree on this. Killer *(reading from an index card),* if you were guaranteed no one would catch you, would you murder a complete stranger for one million dollars?

*(Killer takes his knife and draws it across his throat in the international sign for "dead meat.")*

**Matt:** Who am I kidding? You'd do it for free. Quentin?

**Quentin:** Sure. It's just one person.

**Matt:** Candy?

**Candy:** I'd kill 'em and give the money to charity.

**Matt:** How sweet. OK *(to Contestant),* it's up to you. Do you go with the flow?

**Contestant:** You people are insane! No, I would not kill the person.

*(Killer brandishes his knife and takes a threatening step toward the Contestant. Matt stops him.)*

**Matt:** Sorry, killer, no murders on the show.

*(Killer storms off stage.)*

**Quentin:** This is the lamest thing I've ever done. I'm firing my publicist right now. *(Quentin leaves.)*

**Candy:** *(To Contestant)* We hardly have any money for charity. How can you be so heartless? *(Candy leaves in tears.)*

**Matt:** Well, you've ruined the show. What do you have to say for yourself?

**Contestant:** I guess you have to do the right thing and go against the flow sometimes.

*(Option: Fade up the PowerPoint slide for* Go With the Flow! *and the theme song sound effect.)*

**Matt:** Whatever helps you sleep at night. Sorry for the show today, folks. We'll find someone more willing to go with the flow next time. See you tomorrow on *Go With the Flow!*

## Discussion Questions—Peer Pressure

- Have you ever been pressured to "go with the flow" as the contestant was?

- How do you typically deal with peer pressure?

- Read aloud 1 Corinthians 10:12-13. Do you think you always have a way out of peer pressure? Why or why not?

- In what ways does God gives you strength to stand firm against pressure?

- What areas of your life seem weak when it comes to resisting temptation?

- How can we help one another overcome these traps?

## Discussion Questions—Integrity

- How did the contestant exhibit integrity? Explain.

- Who are some people you know who have integrity? What gives them that characteristic?

- Read aloud Amos 5:10. Why don't people respond well when faced with integrity?

- How can you prepare yourself now so that you will react with integrity when you face future challenges?

- Could areas of your life use more integrity right now? How can you turn things around this week?

# Gray Matter

## Themes

- Absolute Truth (3 John 2-4)
- Sharing Your Faith (1 Peter 3:14-16)

## The Cast

**Francis:** Slick game show host dressed in a suit

**Danny:** Guy's guy, wearing shorts, flip-flops, and a ratty T-shirt

**Halle:** Young woman in business-casual clothes

## The Setting:

A game show. To create this scene, place one podium, angled toward the crowd, on one side of the stage. On the other side, place two podiums, side by side, angled toward the crowd, but facing the first podium. (Use chairs if you can't find three podiums.) Place a dry-erase board, pen, and eraser behind each of the two contestant podiums. Place index cards, with the trivia questions and answers written on them, on the game show host's podium.

## Props and Costumes:

Two dry-erase boards with dry-erase pens, two dry-erase board erasers, three podiums, index cards with the trivia questions written on them, a suit, shorts, flip-flops, ratty T-shirt, and a business-casual outfit

## Media Option:

Use theme music, tense music (to be played while contestants consider and write their answers), and a PowerPoint slide that reads, "Gray Matter." You could also create PowerPoint slides that show the trivia questions and correct answers.

*Francis stands behind his podium. Halle and Danny are offstage.*

*Option: Show the PowerPoint slide for* Gray Matter, *and play the theme music to introduce the scene. Fade the slide and music during Francis' introduction.*

*The scene begins as Francis addresses the audience.*

**Francis:** Good evening and welcome once again to *Gray Matter,* the game show that tests the mysterious space between your ears—your brain. My name is Francis Jones, and we have two new contestants tonight, so let's meet them!

*(Danny and Halle run onstage to join Francis at his podium.)*

**Francis:** Hello, Danny. Thanks for joining us.

**Danny:** It's a dream come true, Fran.

**Francis:** Francis. Call me Francis. Tell our viewers a little bit about yourself there, Danny boy.

**Danny:** I have to say hello to my family. *(Waves.)* I'm really here!

**Francis:** Hurry up, Danny.

**Danny:** Sorry. *(Waves to imaginary camera again.)* They're watching right now.

**Francis:** How precious. *(Turns abruptly.)* And your challenger today is Halle. I understand you're a student.

**Halle:** That's right, Francis. I'm on scholarship at State U, go Salamanders!

**Francis:** Maybe all those book smarts will come in handy today as we test your gray matter. Let's play!

*(They cross to their podiums.)*

**Francis:** The game is simple. I ask a question, and you write down your answer. You get ten points for every answer you get correct. Whoever has the most points at the end of the show wins. Ready?

**Danny and Halle:** We're ready!

**Francis:** Great! First question. *(Reading from an index card)* What country borders the United States to the north?

*(Francis waits for Danny and Halle to write their answers on their dry-erase boards.)*

**Francis:** Please show us your answers.

*(Danny and Halle display their answers to the audience. Halle's answer is "Canada" and Danny's is "Mexico.")*

**Francis:** Canada is correct, Halle. You get ten points! I'm sorry, Danny, but Mexico borders the U.S. to the south.

**Danny:** That depends, Francis.

**Francis:** Excuse me?

**Danny:** North depends on where I'm standing. I mean, people *say* what direction they *believe* north to be, but have they ever been there? Have you ever been there, Francis?

**Francis:** No.

**Danny:** Exactly. So north for me is the direction I'm pointing *(pointing south),* and right now, I'm pointing toward Mexico. That's why Mexico borders the U.S. to the north.

**Francis:** I guess you're right then, Danny. Congratulations, you're tied with ten points!

**Halle:** What? That's ridiculous! The north pole determines where north is.

**Danny:** My north pole is in Brazil.

**Francis:** He's got you there, Halle. Next question. *(Reading from an index card)* What color is the sky?

*(Francis waits for Danny and Halle to write their answers.)*

**Francis:** Please show us your answers.

*(Danny and Halle display their answers to the audience. Halle's answer is "blue" and Danny's is "green.")*

**Francis:** Blue is correct, Halle. You now have twenty points! Come on, Danny, the sky is obviously blue, not green.

**Danny:** I'm colorblind. It looks green to me.

**Francis:** Whoa! Never thought of that. We're tied!

**Halle:** He's not right because he's colorblind. What if I said the sky's black because I'm looking at night or it's brown 'cause I live where there's lots of pollution?

**Francis:** All of those answers are equally correct, Halle. We've got to write better questions—like this one! Who won the 1989 NCAA basketball championship?

*(Francis waits for Danny and Halle to write their answers.)*

**Francis:** Please show us your answers.

*(Halle and Danny display their answers to the audience. Halle's answer is "Michigan" and Danny's is "Seton Hall.")*

**Francis:** Michigan is correct! Halle, you really do have the lead this time with thirty points.

**Danny:** I have to disagree, Francis.

**Francis:** Michigan defeated Seton Hall 80 to 79 in overtime, Danny. The answer's pretty black and white.

**Danny:** I know what the score was, but the moral victory went to Seton Hall. Michigan was heavily favored, and Seton Hall was a complete joke. By making the finals and almost *(makes quotes with his hands)* "winning" the game, Seton Hall placed first in people's hearts. So Seton Hall went down in memory as the real winner.

**Francis:** Good point, Danny. Wow! I guess we're tied once again.

**Halle:** That's not fair! He got the question wrong.

**Francis:** There's no reason to use such harsh language. Children are watching.

**Halle:** Danny is incorrect, mistaken, erroneous, inaccurate, off the mark, less than perfect, short of the goal line, not in the same ballpark, absolutely wrong.

**Danny:** Someone's being a little intolerant.

*(Halle takes a few steps toward Danny as if she's going to hit him.)*

**Halle:** I'll show you...

*(Francis stops Halle.)*

**Francis:** Halle! Please. Let's settle this with your *(taps his head)* gray matter, not your fists.

*(Halle returns to her podium.)*

**Francis:** We'll decide this game by sudden death. Whoever gets the next answer right wins. Fair enough?

**Danny:** I'm game.

**Halle:** *(Mutters.)* I guess so.

**Francis:** Good! Here's the question. *(Reading from index card)* What year did Napoleon Bonaparte die?

*(Francis waits for Danny and Halle to write their answers.)*

**Francis:** Please show us your answers.

*(Danny and Francis display their answers to the audience. Danny's answer is "1809" and Halle's is "1821.")*

**Francis:** Halle wins!

**Danny:** I can't believe a woman picked 1821.

**Halle:** Excuse me?

**Danny:** Napoleon's *body* died in 1821, but every woman knows his heart and spirit died in 1809 when he divorced his wife, Josephine. He loved her passionately, but she couldn't produce an heir, so they divorced. Sure, his body walked around for twelve more years, but Napoleon was dead inside.

**Francis:** I can't argue there. We're tied once again. You know, Halle, you shouldn't be so literal about everything. Take a step to the left or right, and you see things from a different perspective.

*(Halle steps toward Danny.)*

**Halle:** How's this for perspective? I'm going to literally kill Danny for being an idiot. *(Halle starts strangling Danny.)*

**Francis:** That's it, Halle! Loosen up your gray matter.

**Danny:** *(Choking)* She's...killing...me.

**Halle:** No I'm not! From my perspective, this is a deep-tissue body massage.

**Francis:** Ooooh. I'm next! We're out of time, folks. Join us again tomorrow for another test of your *Gray Matter*!

# Discussion Questions—Absolute Truth

- Do you think there is such a thing as absolute truth? Why or why not?

- What do you believe to be true for all people across all times and cultures?

- Read aloud 3 John 2-4. What does "walking in the truth" mean in everyday life?

- Have you ever argued with someone who didn't agree with the truth? What happened?

- How can you reveal truth to people without making them angry?

- In what ways can you begin walking in truth?

# Discussion Questions—Sharing Your Faith

- What would you have done if you were Halle on *Gray Matter*?

- Have you ever had a discussion with someone who believed the exact opposite of what you believed? How did you feel?

- Is it possible to share your faith with someone who disagrees with your ideas? Why or why not?

- Read aloud 1 Peter 3:14-16. How does showing "gentleness and respect" to someone who disagrees with you share your faith?

- How can you display your faith to others without using words?

- Who can you share your faith with this week, and how will you do it?

# The Injustice League

## Themes

- Racism and Prejudice (Galatians 3:27-29)
- Judging (Matthew 7:1-2)

## The Cast

**Batman:** Someone dressed as the traditional superhero, with mask and suit
**Spiderman:** Someone dressed as the traditional superhero, with mask and suit
**The Hulk:** Someone dressed as the traditional superhero, with mask and suit
**Superman:** Someone dressed as the traditional superhero, with suit

## The Setting:

An office. To create this scene, set out a table and four chairs, three on one side of the table and one on the other. Decorate the office with superhero posters and memorabilia. On the table, pile files, folders, papers, and pens.

## Props and Costumes:

Files, folders, papers, pens, superhero action figures, posters, memorabilia, table, chairs, Batman mask and costume, Spiderman mask and costume, Incredible Hulk mask (or green face paint) and costume, and Superman costume

*Batman, Spiderman, and the Hulk are seated behind the long table. Each has a pen and a file with several papers open before him. Batman has a paper in his hand. Superman is offstage.*

*The scene begins when Batman puts the paper down on the table.*

**Batman:** This is hopeless. We'll never find someone to fill Wolverine's place.

**Spiderman:** Why did we interview Captain Loogie? His name says it all.

**Batman:** We're desperate.

**The Hulk:** We shouldn't waste time on people who claim bodily functions as superpowers.

**Batman:** You're just jealous you can't spit through your mask.

*(They laugh at Spiderman.)*

**Spiderman:** I can. I just don't want to.

**The Hulk:** Sure you can. And I can do ballet.

**Batman:** Focus, guys! The next application looks perfect, so pay attention. *(Calls out.)* Next!

*(Superman walks in and shakes hands with Batman.)*

**Superman:** Thanks for seeing me. My name's Superman, alias Clark Kent.

**Batman:** We're so glad you could make it, Mr. Superman. Please, have a seat.

**Superman:** Thank you.

*(Superman introduces himself to the other three superheroes sitting behind the table,*
*shakes their hands, and smiles. Superman sits in the chair across the table facing his interviewers.)*

**Batman:** I'll be honest, your application is impeccable.

**Superman:** Thank you.

**Batman:** We just have a few questions to see if your personality will gel with our crime-fighting team.

**Superman:** Sounds great.

**Spiderman:** I'll start. What exactly are your superpowers?

**Superman:** I have quite a few. I have super-strength, leap tall buildings in a single bound, run faster than a speeding bullet, see through walls, umm…oh yeah, I can fly.

**The Hulk:** First class or coach?

*(The Hulk chuckles at his lame humor. He stops laughing when he notices Batman and Spiderman staring at him.)*

**The Hulk:** Right…um… When was the last time you helped someone?

**Superman:** I saved a school bus yesterday.

**Batman:** And people were inside, right?

**Superman:** Yes, of course.

*(Batman, Spiderman, and the Hulk murmur their approval as they take down some notes.)*

**Batman:** Any weaknesses?

**Superman:** I'm powerless when I come into contact with a substance called kryptonite.

**Batman:** Don't worry. Everybody's got a weakness.

**The Hulk:** I can't stay away from Haagen-Dazs myself.

**Spiderman:** *(Ignoring the Hulk)* So where ya from?

**Superman:** Krypton.

**Spiderman:** That up north somewhere?

**Superman:** Outer space, actually. I'm from a different planet.

*(The interviewers sit back and glance at one another uncomfortably, writing notes.)*

**Batman:** So…you're like an *alien*?

**Superman:** That's correct.

**The Hulk:** *(Nervously)* What brings you to Earth?

**Superman:** Krypton was destroyed and I'm the only survivor. Good thing I like it here 'cause I'm stuck.

*(Superman laughs and the others chuckle politely, but not convincingly.)*

**Superman:** I love the people of Earth. I have some special abilities and want to use them to make life better for people. I really want to help you guys fight crime and make the world a better place.

*(Batman stands and leads Superman to an imaginary door.)*

**Batman:** That's what we like to hear. I think we're done here. There's a couple more applicants we're talking to, so we'll call you when we finish.

**Superman:** There's no more questions?

**The Hulk:** I think we've got it.

*(Superman stands uncertainly.)*

**Superman:** Thank you for your time. If you think of anything else, my pager number and e-mail are on my résumé.

**Spiderman:** Don't call us, we'll call you.

*(Superman walks offstage, closing an imaginary door behind him. The three superheroes relax visibly and exhale deeply.)*

**The Hulk:** Bum-mer. He was perfect!

**Spiderman:** Too good to be true.

**Batman:** Shh! *(Whispers loudly.)* He probably has superhearing.

*(All three huddle together and whisper.)*

**The Hulk:** I can't trust him.

**Spiderman:** He's not human!

**Batman:** Maybe he's OK.

**Spiderman:** Come on, bat brain. You know about aliens, don't you? They steal.

**The Hulk:** Yeah, and they lie about everything.

**Batman:** I've heard they're lazy and never clean up.

**The Hulk:** And they smell like gym socks.

*(Batman and Spiderman look at the Hulk.)*

**The Hulk:** OK, I'm exaggerating. I'm not working with an alien though. He's a freak!

**Batman:** Fine. We'll keep looking.

**Spiderman:** Who's next?

(Batman checks his list.)

**Batman:** Says here, "Whiner Woman."

**The Hulk:** Wonder Woman?

**Batman:** No, *Whiner* Woman. She drives bad guys crazy by constantly whining.

(Spiderman and the Hulk moan.)

**Spiderman:** Not a girl.

**The Hulk:** What about Sloth Boy? He wasn't so bad.

**Spiderman:** He did have a cool costume.

**Batman:** (Calls out.) Next!

## Discussion Questions—Racism and Prejudice

- Why was it silly for the superheroes to be so prejudiced against Superman?

- What racist or prejudiced stereotypes have you heard people use? What examples of racism have you seen in church? at school? at home?

- What are the root causes of racism and prejudice?

- Read aloud Galatians 3:27-29. How should Christians respond to racism and prejudice?

- How can you purge your mind of racist or prejudiced attitudes?

- In what practical ways can you fight racism and prejudice in your community?

## Discussion Questions—Judging

- How was Superman being judged?

- Have you ever been judged unfairly for something? What happened?

- Why do people naturally jump to judging one another?

- Read aloud Matthew 7:1-2. What are the results of judging someone else or of being judged?

- How would you need to change your life if you judged yourself by the standards you have for others?

- In your life, who have you been judgmental toward? How can you change your attitude?

# It's Malachi!

## Themes

- Bible Study (Psalm 119:105-106)
- Heaven (John 14:1-4)

## The Cast

**Kevin:** Regular guy in a snowboarding outfit

**Malachi:** The minor prophet, dressed very "biblically" in a robe with a fake beard

**Abe Lincoln:** The sixteenth president of the United States wearing his traditional beard and stovepipe hat, but also wearing tennis clothes

## The Setting:

Heaven. To create this scene, spread wadded up white sheets or tablecloths around the floor.

## Props and Costumes:

A tennis racket, white sheets or tablecloths, a snowboarding outfit, two fake beards, a robe, a tennis outfit, a stovepipe hat

## Media Option:

Use a recording of the "Hallelujah Chorus" as a sound effect.

*Kevin lies on the ground, as if unconscious, in the center of the stage. Malachi is kneeling beside Kevin. Abraham Lincoln is offstage.*

*Option: Softly play the "Hallelujah Chorus," and have it slowly fade away as the dialogue starts.*

*The scene begins as Malachi gently shakes Kevin.*

**Malachi:** Hey, Kevin, wake up.

*(Kevin stirs and slowly sits up.)*

**Kevin:** What happened? Where am I?

**Malachi:** What's the last thing you remember?

**Kevin:** I dropped into the tree line snowboarding and caught some insane air off this cliff. Must've been twenty feet.

**Malachi:** Try fifty.

**Kevin:** Fifty feet! I coulda died!

**Malachi:** You did.

**Kevin:** What? *(Looks around.)* Hey, where's the snow?

**Malachi:** I'm here to give you your orientation of heaven.

**Kevin:** Heaven? You mean…*(Kevin climbs to his feet and looks around.)*

**Malachi:** Kevin "The K Man" Wells, as one of God's minor prophets, I, Malachi, hereby welcome you with open arms into God's heavenly kingdom.

**Kevin:** I can't believe it! I mean, I knew I was going to heaven, but, this is crazy. *(Pause.)* Hey—wasn't Peter supposed to meet me at the gates?

**Malachi:** Only in the movies.

*(Abraham Lincoln, with beard and stovepipe hat, enters dressed for tennis, complete with racket. Kevin stares at him with his mouth open the whole time.)*

**Abe:** Hey, Malachi. Don't forget we have doubles at two.

**Malachi:** I remember. We're taking those Sons of Thunder down today!

**Abe:** We'll make 'em sit at our right and left after the match tonight. Later! *(Abraham Lincoln leaves.)*

**Kevin:** That was…I can't believe it!

**Malachi:** You'll be a little star struck for a few millennia, but it wears off after a while. *(Pause.)* So, I gotta ask you something.

**Kevin:** You mean you don't just know everything?

**Malachi:** I'm not God here, just a minor prophet. I'm just curious what you thought of my book.

**Kevin:** Your book?

**Malachi:** Yeah. I'd love some constructive criticism.

*(Kevin stares blankly at Malachi.)*

**Malachi:** I'm sorry, you probably didn't catch my name. Heaven can be pretty overwhelming at first. My name's Malachi, and I wrote one of the books of the Bible.

**Kevin:** *(Obviously pretending)* Riiight. I loved it! It had all of those, um…prophecies and Bible verses. Great stuff.

**Malachi:** Really? Do you think so? Looking back I'm afraid it might've come off a little stuffy. How did you like the intro?

**Kevin:** Come on! The intro was great! I mean, I must've read it a million times and it always spoke to me.

**Malachi:** Well, I did have a good ghostwriter. *(Punches Kevin playfully.)* Get it? Ghostwriter! I crack myself up.

**Kevin:** So, can you show me around?

**Malachi:** Sure! Lots to see and all of eternity to see it. One last thing, though. What was the most important thing you got out of my book?

*(Kevin racks his brain for an answer, any answer.)*

**Kevin:** I, uh, thought the most important thing in your book, um…Mal-a-fromumph… *(Kevin trails off, not really remembering Malachi's name.)*

**Malachi:** Malachi.

**Kevin:** That's what I said. Malachi, your book taught me about… *(long dramatic pause)* Jesus.

**Malachi:** What?

**Kevin:** Your book taught me so much about Jesus.

**Malachi:** It's got nothing to do with Jesus! Did you even read my book?

*(Kevin drops his head in shame.)*

**Kevin:** No, I didn't.

**Malachi:** How about the rest of the Old Testament?

**Kevin:** I saw *Prince of Egypt* five times.

**Malachi:** So you devoted your life to God, followed his Son's life and teachings, and didn't even read what he told you to do?

**Kevin:** I read the important stuff.

**Malachi:** I guess that means not *everything* God said was important.

*(Kevin is silent, searching for an excuse.)*

**Kevin:** Can you plead the Fifth up here?

# Discussion Questions—Bible Study

- Would you be in the same boat as Kevin if you went to heaven right now? Why or why not?

- What reasons do you have for not studying the Bible more?

- Read aloud Psalm 119:105-106. What are the benefits of reading and knowing the Bible?

- When have you personally experienced some of these benefits?

- What practical steps can you take to learn more about the Bible?

## Discussion Questions—Heaven

- Do you think you'll be quizzed in heaven on your Bible knowledge? Why or why not?

- What parts of the drama were inaccurate about heaven?

- What are some popular images of heaven that we get from movies and TV?

- Read aloud John 14:1-4. What does Jesus' description tell you about heaven? Why do you think he doesn't give the disciples a lot of details?

- What do we know for certain about heaven?

- How does your belief in heaven affect how you live your life today?

# *Just Listen*

## Themes

- Hearing God (Jeremiah 33:3)
- Impure Motives (Acts 5:1-11)

## The Cast

**Bryce:** Teenage boy

**Nick:** Teenage boy

**Tim:** Teenage boy

**Jesus:** Son of God, wearing a white robe

## The Setting:

A church pew facing the audience

## Props and Costumes:

A Bible, a megaphone, and a white robe

## Media Option:

Use a recording of one of your pastor's sermons—one about Moses is best.

*Bryce, Nick, and Tim sit on the church pew. Jesus kneels behind the pew. Bryce has a closed Bible on his lap and the megaphone is hidden behind the pew.*

*Option: Softly play the sermon tape throughout the drama.*

*The scene begins when Bryce first speaks.*

**Bryce:** This is so boring!

**Nick:** Why doesn't Jesus just talk to us himself instead of us having to listen to these stupid sermons?

*(Jesus appears behind the boys. The boys do not acknowledge or react to Jesus' presence throughout the drama.)*

**Tim:** He probably wouldn't want to talk to us anyway.

**Jesus:** I'm right here, Tim.

**Bryce:** *(Gesturing toward his Bible)* I need something more than this stupid old book to read! I can't understand it.

**Jesus:** You never try to read it. *(Jesus opens the Bible in Bryce's lap and points to a verse.)* Try this verse right here.

**Bryce:** How did that get open? *(Bryce closes the Bible.)*

**Tim:** Listen to this guy go on and on and on about Moses.

**Jesus:** Moses is such a stud.

**Tim:** It must've been easy for Moses to believe. He had God talk to him all the time, and he showed up in a burning bush and stuff.

**Jesus:** Look around you! The sun rises every day, babies are born, I've given you health and a place to live and food to eat. I'm right here, if only you'd just listen to me!

**Nick:** I wish my parents didn't make me come here every single Sunday.

**Bryce:** You lie. You'd come just to see Vanessa.

**Nick:** Yeah. Vanessa seems to get a lot out of church, though.

**Jesus:** She spends a lot of time talking to me. She even mentioned you when we were hanging out. I've got some advice for you, if only you'd just be quiet enough to let me get a word in!

**Bryce:** If Jesus really cared, he would have helped me in my baseball game last night. I struck out three times!

**Jesus:** I do care, Bryce. But you didn't want to glorify me. You wanted to impress Jessica.

**Nick:** Jessica wasn't very impressed. I think she wants to go out with Tom now.

*(Jesus jumps in front of the boys and wildly waves his arms, but the boys don't react.)*

**Jesus:** I can help you! Just listen to me for once! I love you guys so much!

**Tim:** Who cares about a stupid baseball game? I made a D minus on that test last week. Praying didn't help one bit.

**Jesus:** Praying after you turn the test in is a little late. Let's talk about it *before*hand, or even during it. And I'd like to really *talk*— not only when you want something. You know, *talk*? communicating back and forth?

**Bryce:** My grandma's always griping at me for not reading my Bible. She may need all of that stuff, but I've got my whole life ahead of me. I just want to have fun for a while!

*(Jesus pulls out a megaphone and points it at the boys' heads.)*

**Jesus:** Please listen to me for one second! I could tell you how to have an abundant life now!

*(Option: fade out sermon tape.)*

**Tim:** Finally! That was the longest sermon in history.

**Bryce:** Let's go.

**Nick:** I sure hope there's donuts today. I'm starving.

*(The boys leave Jesus alone.)*

**Jesus:** I wonder if they would hear me better if Dad had made them with four ears?

## Discussion Questions—Hearing God

- Does God speak to people today the way he did in the Bible? Why or why not?

- Do you think God has ever spoken to you? If so, how did you know it was God? If not, why not?

- Read aloud Jeremiah 33:3. Do you believe this verse is true? Why or why not?

- In what ways can God answer your prayers and questions?

- What makes it hard to hear God when he speaks?

- How can you learn to hear God more clearly in your life?

## Discussion Questions—Impure Motives

- What were the boys' motives for going to church or praying?

- Why do people think they can use Jesus for whatever they want?

- Read aloud Acts 5:1-11. Why did God kill these people?

- Why do you think God cares so much about people's motives if they're doing good things on the outside?

- What should motivate us when we're working for God or coming before him with requests?

- How can you develop pure motives when you approach God?

# Loose Lips

## Themes

- Gossip (Proverbs 16:27-28)
- Trust (Proverbs 25:19)

## The Cast

**Kami:** Teenage girl
**Beth:** Teenage girl
**Hope:** Teenage girl

## The Setting:

Three bedrooms. The center stage area is Kami's bedroom where she sits at a desk studying her books. Beth lies on her bed at stage left, and Hope sits on the floor at stage right painting her toenails.

## Props:

Three telephones, a desk, chair, books, nail polish, bed, pillow

## Media Option:

Use a ringing telephone sound effect.

*Kami is frozen, sitting and studying in her "room" at center stage. Beth is frozen, lying on her bed and holding the telephone at stage left. Hope is frozen, holding a telephone receiver against her ear and painting her toenails at stage right.*

*Option: Play the ringing telephone sound effect to begin the skit.*

*The scene begins as Kami and Beth unfreeze. Kami picks up the telephone and speaks.*

**Kami:** Hello?

**Beth:** Hey, Kami. It's Beth.

**Kami:** Beth! What's up?

**Beth:** Just finished my chemistry. How about you?

**Kami:** Trying to decipher my algebra. Hey, isn't Hope in your chemistry class?

**Beth:** Yeah, she sits right next to me.

**Kami:** I heard that she called you a big, lying back stabber.

**Beth:** What for?

**Kami:** She said you were talking about her to Robert and he told all of his friends and now the whole school knows.

**Beth:** I can't believe she'd say that! I've never said a word about Hope to Robert. She's one of my best friends!

**Kami:** Why would she say that?

**Beth:** She's probably jealous.

**Kami:** Oh! Could you hold on? That's my other line. *(Kami clicks over.)* Hello?

*(Beth hugs her pillow tight. Hope unfreezes and begins painting her toenails as she talks on the phone.)*

**Hope:** Hey, Kami. You done studying yet?

**Kami:** Hope! Not quite. You will never guess what I heard today.

**Hope:** What?

**Kami:** Beth is telling everyone you're jealous of her and Robert.

**Hope:** Jealous? of her and Robert? I think Robert's a nice guy, but he's not my type.

**Kami:** You're right. Could you hang on for a sec? I've got someone on the other line.

**Hope:** Sure.

**Kami:** Thanks. *(Kami clicks over.)* Beth, you still there?

**Beth:** Yes.

**Kami:** I've got to tell you what else Hope is saying.

**Beth:** There's more?

**Kami:** She's telling everybody that Robert is the biggest loser to ever go to our school. Can you believe it?

**Beth:** A loser? Maybe she could talk if she'd ever actually had a boyfriend. I don't know why she didn't just come talk to me.

**Kami:** Who knows. Let me get this other person off the line, OK? Hang on. *(Kami clicks over.)* Hope?

**Hope:** I'm here.

**Kami:** I just heard something else.

**Hope:** What now?

**Kami:** Beth thinks you couldn't get a date if you were the last woman on earth!

**Hope:** I can't believe that! We were such good friends. I sit by her in chemistry.

**Kami:** Really?

**Hope:** Yeah. I can't figure out why she'd turn on me. I've got to be more careful choosing my friends.

**Kami:** I'm your friend, Hope.

**Hope:** I know, Kam. I gotta eat dinner. See you tomorrow. *(Hope hangs up and shakes her head. She walks offstage calling out)* Mom!

You won't believe what I just found out!

**Kami:** *(Kami clicks over.)* Beth?

**Beth:** Did you get rid of them?

**Kami:** Yes.

**Beth:** Thanks for being honest with me, Kami. I want to know if someone's spreading rumors about me.

**Kami:** You would do the same for me.

**Beth:** I've got to go. Good luck with the algebra.

**Kami:** Thanks.

*(Both girls hang up. Beth starts to cry. Kami giggles to herself and starts on her homework again.)*

## Discussion Questions—Gossip

- What is the most recent piece of gossip you've heard? Was it true?

- What is the difference between "gossip" and "information"?

- What makes gossip so appealing?

- Read aloud Proverbs 16:27-28. When has gossip been dangerous for you or someone you know? What happened?

- What are the benefits of being part of gossip? What are the negative consequences?

- In what ways can you stop gossip in its tracks?

## Discussion Questions—Trust

- Why did the girls in the drama trust Kami?

- What does it take for someone to gain your trust?

- Read aloud Proverbs 25:19. Have you ever trusted the wrong person? What happened?

- How can you discern whether someone is trustworthy?

- How can you make yourself more trustworthy?

# One More Thing

## Themes

- Facing Temptation (James 1:14-16)
- Premarital Sex (1 Corinthians 6:18-20)

## The Cast

**Jordan:** Teenage boy

**Hillary:** Teenage girl

**Carny:** Creepy-looking guy in grubby jeans, white tank undershirt, and backward baseball cap

**Girl:** Teenage girl

## The Setting:

A Ferris wheel. To create this scene, place a bench (or pew) in the middle of the stage.

## Props and Costumes:

Cotton candy, stuffed animal, a bench, grubby jeans, white tank undershirt, baseball cap

## Media Option:

Use video footage of a carnival.

*Carny is onstage next to the empty carriage of a Ferris wheel (the bench). Jordan and Hillary are offstage. Jordan has the cotton candy and Hillary carries the stuffed animal throughout the drama. The Girl is offstage.*

*Option: Play the carnival footage to introduce the scene.*

*The scene begins as Hillary and Jordan walk onstage, silently talking to each other.*

**Carny:** Step right up. Don't be shy! No heart can resist the ride of your life on the Ferris wheel!

*(Jordan, eating the cotton candy, and Hillary walk up to Carny.)*

**Carny:** Good evening, sir! How are you, madame?

**Hillary:** *(Giggles.)* Fine.

**Jordan:** We want to ride the Ferris wheel.

**Carny:** It's your lucky night. We've got one right here! Hop in.

*(Hillary and Jordan take their seats in the Ferris wheel.)*

**Carny:** Are you two ready to have the best time of your life?

**Jordan and Hillary:** Yeah!

**Carny:** I can't hear you.

**Jordan and Hillary:** YEAH!!!

**Carny:** Great. Have fun! *(Pause.)* Before you go, I should let you know a few things.

**Jordan:** Like what?

**Carny:** Your ride might have a few surprises.

**Hillary:** It's a Ferris wheel. It goes around and around in a big circle.

**Carny:** Then you don't have anything to worry about, do you? I'm just supposed to tell you that riding the Ferris wheel may cause nausea.

**Jordan:** No sweat.

**Carny:** And it *can* make you sweat, ya know— scare ya pretty bad.

**Hillary:** I love danger.

**Carny:** You go girl!

*(Carny and Hillary high five.)*

**Carny:** Then you won't care that this ride can also cause dry mouth, bloating, migraines, halitosis, vertigo, scurvy, cysts, and explosive bowel movements.

**Hillary:** You're kidding.

**Carny:** Serious as a heart attack, which can also be caused by this ride.

**Jordan:** *(Laughing)* That stuff doesn't really happen. Quit trying to scare us, man.

**Carny:** Sure it does. All the time.

**Hillary:** How often does it happen?

**Carny:** Look, if you want statistics you can watch ESPN. I just know how to run the Ferris wheel.

*(The Girl walks up while Carny is talking and taps him on the shoulder when he's finished speaking.)*

**Girl:** Excuse me?

**Carny:** Sorry, you'll have to wait your turn.

**Girl:** I think I left my purse here last night.

**Carny:** I remember you! How's your boyfriend?

**Girl:** Not so good. He's in ICU.

**Carny:** Oh, I'm sorry. Tough break.

**Girl:** You warned us, but we couldn't resist. *(Pause.)* My purse?

**Carny:** Oh, yeah! It's in the lost and found at the ticket booth.

**Girl:** Thanks. See ya!

*(The Girl leaves, and Carny turns back to Jordan and Hillary.)*

**Hillary:** Who was that?

**Carny:** Just a girl who rode the Ferris wheel.

**Jordan:** What happened to her boyfriend?

**Carny:** He rode too.

**Jordan:** And he went to the hospital?

**Carny:** Yup.

*(Jordan and Hillary look at each other.)*

**Carny:** You guys can get off. No one's putting a gun to your head.

**Hillary:** It's cool. I really want to go.

**Jordan:** Yeah, it's not like anyone's died riding the Ferris wheel.

*(Carny is silent.)*

**Jordan:** Someone died?

**Carny:** It's happened on occasion.

**Hillary:** Does occasion mean once every ten years or once a month?

**Carny:** Yes.

**Jordan:** Which is it?

**Carny:** I just run the ride, OK? You don't have to do it.

**Jordan:** No, I'm down with riding. I'm just trying to get as much info as possible.

**Carny:** You sure?

**Jordan:** I'll try anything once.

**Hillary:** We're ready for anything. Besides, the chances of anything happening are pretty slim.

**Carny:** You're the boss. Enjoy your ride, and don't look down!

## Discussion Questions—Facing Temptation

- Why do you think the couple found riding the Ferris wheel tempting?

- Why do you think Jordan and Hillary decided to ride it even though it was so dangerous?

- Do you believe you can be tempted to give in to sin without realizing it? Why or why not?

- Read aloud James 1:14-16. What steps are involved in temptation?

- What types of temptation are really hard to resist? Why are they so hard to resist?

- How can you guard yourself against temptation, so you don't even think about riding the "Ferris wheel"?

# Discussion Questions—Premarital Sex

- Do you think the couple was wrong for *wanting* to ride the Ferris wheel? Why or why not?

- Pretend riding the Ferris wheel represents participating in premarital sex. At what point did Hillary and Jordan cross the line into sin?

- Are sexual desires a sin? Why or why not?

- Read aloud 1 Corinthians 6:18-20. Why would God prohibit premarital sex if he created sex to be "good"?

- How can a Christian deal with sexual urges in the right way?

# One Willing Monk

### (Based on the true story of the martyr Telemachus)

## Themes

- Sacrifice (1 John 3:16)
- Following God's Will (Matthew 22:35-40)

## The Cast

**Tim:** Monk dressed in a robe

**Brandonius:** Roman dressed in a toga

**Gladiator 1:** Gladiator dressed for combat in a helmet, white T-shirt, shorts, and sandals

**Gladiator 2:** Gladiator dressed for combat in a helmet, white T-shirt, shorts, and sandals

**Bell Ringer:** Person who rings a bell from offstage

## The Setting:

A street and the Roman Coliseum. The street scene is stage right. For the Coliseum, place a bench stage left for Tim and Brandonius to sit on and have the gladiators on the floor below them, so Tim can jump down into the "ring."

## Props and Costumes:

Two swords, a bench, a bell (a hand bell or triangle), a robe, a toga, two helmets, two gladiator outfits

## Media Option:

Use a video clip of the city of Rome from the movie *Gladiator*.

*Brandonius is center stage. All other characters are offstage. The gladiators have their swords with them offstage.*

*Option: Show the video clip from* Gladiator *to introduce the scene.*

*The scene begins as the bell is rung several times from offstage. Tim walks onstage and taps Brandonius on the shoulder.*

Tim: Excuse me?

Brandonius: Yes.

Tim: Could you please tell me what the bell means?

*(Brandonius looks over Tim's monk robe.)*

Brandonius: You're not from around here.

Tim: I'm a monk.

Brandonius: *(Sarcastically)* Really. I never would've guessed. Anyway, to answer your question, the bell means it's time to go to the Coliseum.

Tim: Can I go with you? I don't know my way around town.

Brandonius: Sure. My name's Brandonius.

Tim: My name's Tim.

*(The two men shake hands and begin to walk back and forth across stage right as if they were walking down city streets.)*

Brandonius: That's your whole name?

Tim: Should there be more?

Brandonius: Everybody has an *ius* at the end of his name. I figured you'd be *Timius*.

Tim: It's just Tim.

Brandonius: OK, What brings you to Rome?

Tim: I've lived in a monastery my entire life until now.

Brandonius: Sounds boring—being stuck in a castle with a bunch of monks.

Tim: Oh, no! I grew up watching the monks' peaceful lives and saw how much they loved God. They taught me that Christ died for my sins, so I decided to join them and learn more about Jesus.

Brandonius: Ixnay on the esus-Jay! He's not too popular round here.

Tim: Why?

Brandonius: People don't like being told what to do. So what does a monk do? pray and make sad faces?

Tim: My favorite thing to do is tell the town's children stories from the Bible. I also have a hobby.

Brandonius: Needlepoint?

Tim: No! I love to read travel books. I've never been outside our little town, so I explored the world through books. When I read about Rome, it was like God told me to come here.

Brandonius: Did he sound like Darth Vader?

Tim: I didn't actually hear him, but I knew he was speaking. Father Joseph said, "If God wants you to leave, I can't make you stay. May God guard you and bless you on your journey." So here I am—glorious Rome.

**Brandonius:** I know that's what the brochures say, but believe me, Rome's not all the hype promises.

**Tim:** I don't care. I'm excited! God's got something for me here. People laughed at me and told me, "Rome is no place for a monk. It is too big." Let me tell you, my God is big enough to use me in Rome if he wants to.

**Brandonius:** You have to admit you stick out in a crowd.

**Tim:** I don't mind. This city's amazing! All of the people and the architecture! I don't know what I can possibly do in this town for God, but I'm sure he'll show me.

*(Tim and Brandonius arrive at the bench.)*

**Brandonius:** Here we are.

**Tim:** The Coliseum is huge!

**Brandonius:** It's fairly new. They built it for the last Olympics. Let's sit here.

**Tim:** OK.

*(Both sit.)*

**Brandonius:** Whoops! Stand up.

*(They stand.)*

**Tim:** What for?

**Brandonius:** And bow. *(Bows and sits.)* It's the emperor.

*(Tim stares in awe at the unseen emperor.)*

**Tim:** This is why God wanted me to come here, so I could see what royalty is like. *(Prays.)* Dear Lord, I praise you for your majesty and for showing me how I should revere you. Amen.

*(While Tim prays, the gladiators come onstage with their swords and take their places in the "ring," facing each other for battle. Tim opens his eyes and sits.)*

**Tim:** Who are those men?

**Brandonius:** Today's contestants. My money's on Peter the Perturbed. *(Aside)* I got an inside tip that his opponent Blutonius the Bludgeon ate some tainted shellfish for lunch. *(To Tim)* Care to make a bet?

**Tim:** Wait. I've read about this.

**Brandonius:** Betting's easy. If my guy wins, I get the money…

**Tim:** I know what betting is. I mean that those are gladiators! They're not going to kill each other, are they?

**Brandonius:** The marque doesn't say, "fight to the death" for nothing.

**Tim:** How can you watch this?

**Brandonius:** It's better than the movie.

**Tim:** This is wrong! I must stop it.

*(Tim stands up and pleads with the gladiators, who circle each other, ready for battle.)*

**Tim:** Please! In the name of Jesus Christ who died for you, you don't have to do this!

**Brandonius:** Tim, sit down. That isn't funny.

**Tim:** No!

(Tim runs down the aisle and jumps into the arena. The two gladiators stand facing each other with swords. Tim runs up to Gladiator 1.)

**Tim:** Please! In the name of Jesus Christ who died for you, you don't have to do this!

(Gladiator 1 shoves Tim to the ground. Tim gets up and approaches Gladiator 2.)

**Tim:** Listen to me! In the name of Jesus Christ who died for you, you don't have to do this!

**Gladiator 2:** Get out of here!

(Gladiator 2 pushes Tim to the side and approaches his opponent. Tim jumps up and rushes between them, speaking to Gladiator 1.)

**Tim:** In the name of Jesus Christ who died for you, you don't have to do this!

(Gladiator 1 stabs Tim with his sword. The gladiators slowly back away and step off-stage as Tim falls to the ground, mortally wounded.)

**Tim:** (Gasping) In the name of Jesus Christ who died for you, you don't have to do this. (Tim dies.)

(Brandonius jumps into the ring and kneels beside Tim. He closes Tim's eyelids and stands.)

**Brandonius:** (To audience) Slowly, after Tim died, a few people got up and left, followed by a few more, followed by the emperor, followed by more, until the Coliseum was completely empty. What you just witnessed was the true story of how Telemachus, one man willing to be used by God, brought about the end of the gladiator fights. Because of his obedience, there was never another gladiator fight in Rome.

# Discussion Questions—Sacrifice

- Do you think you could sacrifice your life for others as Tim did? Why or why not?

- Which people have sacrificed for you? How did their actions affect you?

- Read aloud 1 John 3:16. How does this command stack up against how the world tells people to live?

- Do you fear God will ask you to sacrifice something you don't want to give up? Why or why not?

- In what ways can we lay down our lives for those around us?

# Discussion Questions—Following God's Will

- Can you hear God's voice and know his plan for your life as Tim did? If so, how?

- Read aloud Matthew 22:35-40. How did Tim live out these verses?

- How does living out these verses guarantee that you'll follow God's will for your life?

- Why is it sometimes so natural to focus on God's will for the distant future instead of living each day in obedience?

- How can you live out these verses in your life tomorrow?

# The Reason

## Themes

- Christmas (Luke 2:1-7)
- The Urgency of Following Christ (Isaiah 55:6-7)

## The Cast

**Brianna:** Teenage girl dressed in winter clothes

**Amy:** Teenage girl dressed in winter clothes

**Announcer:** Person who gives in-store announcements with a microphone from offstage

(Optional) **Employee:** Store employee wearing an apron and a name tag

## The Setting:

A department store. To create this scene, put a clearance shelf (or table) at center stage with Christmas decorations and figurines on it. Put a sale sign on the shelf. (Optional: You also could put a revolving light on the table or shelves. Place a shopping cart filled with items at stage right, and place the artificial tree stage left.)

## Props and Costumes:

A microphone, a shelf (or table), Christmas decorations (including one Santa figurine and one Baby Jesus figurine), two shopping bags, a sale sign, winter clothes (Optional: revolving light, an artificial Christmas tree, shopping cart with items in it, apron, name tag)

## Media Option:

Use video footage of the outside of your local mall or discount store.

*Brianna holds a shopping bag as she studies some of the Christmas decorations on display. Amy is offstage with a shopping bag. The Announcer is offstage with a microphone throughout the drama.*

*Option: The Employee is onstage dismantling the artificial Christmas tree throughout the skit. If you do not have a Christmas tree, the Employee can sort and rearrange the various Christmas decorations. Play the video footage of the outside of the store to introduce the drama.*

*The scene begins as the first announcement is made.*

**Announcer:** Remember, shoppers, only 364 more days until Christmas!

*(Amy walks onstage and taps Brianna on the shoulder.)*

**Amy:** Merry Christmas!

*(Brianna, surprised, turns and smiles when she sees Amy.)*

**Brianna:** Amy! Merry Christmas to you, too!

*(The pair quickly hug and separate.)*

**Amy:** Would you believe I saw them putting up Valentine's decorations already?

**Brianna:** Retail never looks back. How was your Christmas?

**Amy:** Really nice. I loved not having to deal with Grandma's abominable fruitcake or Grandpa's never-ending stories without a point.

**Announcer:** Sorry, kids. Pikachu has left the building. Catch a photo if you can with him next Sunday between 3 and 5.

**Brianna:** *(Growling with anger)* I want Pokemon banished to the darkest corner of the island of annoying toys! My brother ran around all day screaming, "Gotta catch 'em all." I honestly wish he'd get into Barney again!

**Amy:** At least he talks to you. My dad and brothers have been grunting and yelling at football games all week.

**Brianna:** What'd you get?

**Amy:** Luggage.

**Brianna:** Ahhhh!! I hate that! I got a set for my birthday.

**Amy:** It gets worse. They gave me the suitcase for Christmas and I get the hanging bag for my birthday.

**Brianna:** It's a simple concept. A Christmas present isn't something you need—it should be something *special*.

**Amy:** Preach it, girl! Presents should be foolish, something you'd never get yourself, or could never afford.

**Announcer:** The white zone is for exchanges only. The red zone is for shopping.

**Amy:** You here to exchange stuff?

**Brianna:** No, Mom wants me to pick up some decorations for next year while they're cheap.

**Amy:** What are you getting?

*(Brianna picks up two decorations. One is Santa, and the other is Baby Jesus.)*

**Brianna:** Help me decide between these two.

**Amy:** Santa and Baby Jesus?

**Brianna:** You've got to be careful. They definitely make different statements.

**Amy:** Which are…

**Brianna:** You know. Santa's jolly, spreads Christmas cheer, and kids love him.

**Amy:** And Jesus is mean, spreads sorrow, and children flee him in terror?

**Brianna:** That's not what I mean! I'm just saying that Jesus can be so…offensive. Christmas is about peace on earth, not ticking people off.

**Amy:** Come on, Brianna. The only offensive babies out there are the ones with overflowing diapers. Besides, the whole Christmas thing is supposed to celebrate his birthday.

**Brianna:** Did you know Christmas is Sam Robinson's birthday, too? He's always complaining about how he gets cheated out of presents that way.

**Announcer:** A white Neon, license plate "PLAYA," your lights are on. Also, your fuzzy dice and cowhide seat covers are extremely tacky.

**Amy:** *(Checks watch.)* I've got to run. I'm supposed to help take the Christmas lights down.

**Brianna:** It's the day after Christmas! You can leave them up until after New Year's.

**Amy:** Dad's so cheap. He can't stand paying for extra electricity. *(Pointing at the decorations)* Still need help?

*(Brianna turns her attention back to the sale rack.)*

**Brianna:** I think I'll go with Santa.

**Amy:** Are you sure? I mean, Baby Jesus is so cute. I'd rather have him than a creepy, fat guy.

**Brianna:** There's always plenty of Jesuses left lying around. I can get him anytime. Besides, if I wait until next week, he'll probably be 75 percent off. Then I'll have the best of both worlds—Santa and Jesus!

**Amy:** Whatever you say. Have a happy New Year!

**Brianna:** You too. I'll see you at Jill's party, OK?

**Amy:** See ya then! *(Amy exits.)*

*(Brianna picks up both the Santa and the Jesus. She studies them and finally puts down Jesus. Brianna exits, leaving Jesus behind.)*

# Discussion Questions—Christmas

- What do you dislike about the Christmas season?

- What is your favorite Christmas memory?

- What does Christmas mean to you?

- Read aloud Luke 2:1-7. Why does the true meaning of Christmas—the birth of Christ—so often get buried under the Christmas rush?

- How can you keep Jesus at the center of the Christmas season?

- In what ways can we point our friends and community to Jesus this year?

## Discussion Questions—The Urgency of Following Christ

- Why did Brianna put off buying the Jesus figurine even though the store might sell out?

- Have you ever missed something important because you procrastinated or dawdled? What happened?

- What reasons do people have for putting off following Christ?

- Read aloud Isaiah 55:6-7. What does this Scripture say about the urgency of choosing to follow God?

- Can you run out of time to follow Jesus? Why or why not?

- Does anything prevent you from following Christ right now?

# Samson 3000

## Themes

- Focus (1 John 2:15-17)
- Talents (Colossians 3:17)

## The Cast

**Samson:** The biblical judge, initially having long hair (a wig) and later a short, stylish haircut. He starts out wearing a toga and sandals and ends up wearing a cool sweat suit and sunglasses.

**Delilah:** Seductive, scheming woman, wearing a red dress and high heels

**Emcee:** Guy in a suit with a slick hairdo

**Stone:** Muscular guy, wearing black pants and a black vest (You also may want to paint his face to look like a professional wrestler.)

**Bones:** Skinny little guy, wearing orange shorts and an orange sweat shirt ten times too big for him

## The Setting:

A wrestling ring. To create this scene, simply keep the stage empty. You also may want to plant some people in the audience to cheer or hold up signs for the wrestlers.

## Props and Costumes:

A microphone, sunglasses, a longhaired wig, a sweat suit, a toga, sandals, a suit, a red dress and high heels, black pants, black vest, orange shorts, orange sweat shirt (Optional: face paint and signs for the audience to hold up)

## Media Option:

Use a video clip from the opening credits of a wrestling program.

*The Emcee is standing center stage with a microphone. Samson and Stone are frozen, in opposite corners of the "ring" near the Emcee. Delilah and Bones are offstage.*

*Option: Play the opening credits for a television wrestling match to introduce the scene.*

*The scene begins as the Emcee starts speaking.*

**Emcee:** Ladies and gentlemen, welcome to tonight's main event. In the right corner, weighing 260 pounds, wearing the black vest and sunglasses, Stone!

*(Stone unfreezes and flexes his muscles a bit.)*

**Emcee:** And tonight's challenger, in the left corner, weighing 180 pounds, wearing a toga, sandals, and long hair, Samson!

*(Samson unfreezes, smiles and waves to the audience. The two contestants walk to the middle by the Emcee and shake hands.)*

**Emcee:** Remember, keep it clean, and no firearms or jawbones of a donkey. Return to your corners.

*(Samson and Stone return to their corners.)*

**Emcee:** It's time to bring on the pain!!!!

*(The Emcee backs away as Samson and Stone come at each other. They meet in the center and struggle for a while, but Samson soon overcomes Stone and pins him to the ground. The Emcee gives the ten count. Samson jumps around in victory, and the Emcee holds up Samson's arm.)*

**Emcee:** Samson is the new champion!

**Stone:** I'll be back.

**Samson:** I just want to thank God for everything he's done for me. Without him I wouldn't have had the strength and the courage to beat such a fine opponent.

*(Stone and the Emcee exit. Samson begins to exit after them when Delilah steps out in front of him.)*

**Delilah:** Congratulations, Samson.

**Samson:** Thank you.

**Delilah:** My name's Delilah, and I think I can help you.

**Samson:** How can you do that?

**Delilah:** Do you have an agent?

**Samson:** No, I just do exactly what God tells me.

**Delilah:** That's gotten you this far, Samson, but have you been able to really enjoy the success that God has blessed you with?

**Samson:** I don't understand.

**Delilah:** Right now, you're the world champion. But you haven't marketed yourself at all. You could be a household name with endorsements and fame with the right image.

**Samson:** I don't think I need any of that. God looks after me.

**Delilah:** Of course he does. But don't you think he wants you to enjoy yourself, too? You've worked so hard for God, and it's time you received a little in return for your time and devotion. Besides, think of all the people who would hear about God if your face was on a Wheaties box!

**Samson:** I don't know.

**Delilah:** At least let me help you find some new clothes. You could use a new image.

*(Samson fingers his toga, embarrassed.)*

**Samson:** It is a little bit old, and it does get really drafty in the winter.

**Delilah:** I'll tell you what—let me take you shopping, make some suggestions on clothes, see if you like my professional advice, and we'll go from there.

**Samson:** OK.

**Delilah:** Fantastic!

*(Delilah hooks her arm through Samson's as they walk away.)*

**Delilah:** I think this could be the start of a beautiful relationship.

*(Offstage Samson puts on a new costume: a sweat suit and sunglasses, and removes the wig. The Emcee with the microphone, Bones, Delilah, and Samson enter. The Emcee stands at center stage while Bones and Samson freeze in their respective corners of the "ring." Delilah freezes next to Samson.)*

**Emcee:** Ladies and gentlemen! Welcome to the main event. This match will determine the wrestling champion of the world! In the red corner, weighing 130 pounds, wearing the orange shorts and sweat shirt, Bones!

*(Bones unfreezes, clasps his hands and shakes them over each shoulder in victory.)*

**Emcee:** And in the white corner, weighing 180 pounds, wearing the designer sweats and sunglasses, the reigning champion of the world, Samson!

*(Samson unfreezes and strikes a bodybuilder pose for the crowd. Delilah claps with delight.)*

**Delilah:** They love the new you, darling!

**Samson:** You're right! I should have cut my hair a long time ago. Now it doesn't get in my face when we drive the convertible.

**Delilah:** Go get him, dear. He's a wimp.

**Samson:** I'll tear him apart.

**Emcee:** Come to the center, gentlemen.

*(Samson and Bones meet in the middle.)*

**Emcee:** OK, men. Let's keep it clean.

**Bones:** *(Jogging in place and throwing a few punches in the air)* I'm a lean, mean fighting machine!

*(Samson and the Emcee double over in belly-shaking laughter. Bones pouts as they keep laughing long and hard. The Emcee finally pulls it together enough to speak.)*

**Emcee:** Return to your corners.

*(Samson and Bones return to their corners.)*

**Emcee:** Bring on the pain!

*(The Emcee steps back as Samson and Bones advance toward each other.)*

**Samson:** I'll tell you what, little man. I'll give you a free shot. *(Pointing to his chin)* Right here on the chin. Go for it.

*(Bones takes a huge swing and hits Samson on the chin. Samson shudders from the impact.)*

**Samson:** Ouch. *(Samson falls to the ground, knocked out cold.)*

**Emcee:** Our new champion! *(The Emcee raises Bones' arm, Delilah runs over and throws her arms around Bones.)*

**Delilah:** You were fantastic!

**Samson:** *(Coming to his senses and sitting up slowly)* What happened? Delilah?

**Bones:** *(Sings)* I am the champion. I am the champion!

*(Delilah leads Bones offstage.)*

**Delilah:** You stick with me, Bones, and I'll make you bigger than Tiger Woods.

*(Samson's head falls back on the floor in defeat.)*

# Discussion Questions—Focus

- How did Samson get distracted from serving God?

- Who are some people you know personally or in the news who have lost their focus on God?

- Why is it sometimes so hard to focus on God?

- Read aloud 1 John 2:15-17. What things distract you from your relationship with God?

- What happens to us when we lose our focus?

- How can you increase your focus on God?

# Discussion Questions—Talents

- Where did Samson go wrong in using God's gift of strength?

- What is your best talent or ability?

- Do you feel you're using it for yourself, or are you using it to bring God glory? Why?

- Read aloud Colossians 3:17. How can you live out this verse? Give some practical ideas and examples.

- Why do you think God gave you the particular talents that he did?

- How can you more effectively use your gifts and talents to glorify God?

# The Switch

## Themes

- Obeying Parents (Proverbs 23:22)
- Stereotypes (John 13:34-35)

## The Cast

**Mom:** Mother dressed in casual clothes

**Dad:** Father dressed for work

**Debbie:** Teen dressed very conservatively in a poodle skirt, bobby socks, and bulky sweater

**Announcer:** Advertising spokesman wearing a suit

## The Setting:

A family breakfast room. To create this scene, place a breakfast table and three chairs in the middle of the stage. Set the table with three plates of food and drinks. Also place an apple and a carton of milk on the table.

## Props and Costumes:

Table and three chairs, three plates of food, three glasses, newspaper, schoolbooks, an apple, a carton of milk, casual women's clothes, two men's suits, a poodle skirt, bobby socks, and a bulky sweater

## Media Option:

Use video footage of the exterior of a house.

*Mom is onstage. Debbie, Dad, and the Announcer are offstage. Debbie holds the schoolbooks, and the newspaper is offstage.*

*Option: Show the video clip of a house to introduce the scene.*

*The scene begins as Mom sets the last plate of food on the table.*

**Mom:** Breakfast's ready!

*(Debbie comes in carrying her schoolbooks looking as if she stepped out of* Happy Days.*)*

**Debbie:** Morning, Mom.

*(Debbie gives her mom a kiss on the cheek, sets her books on the table, and sits down. They freeze. The Announcer enters and steps in front of the table.)*

**Announcer:** Mrs. Jackson doesn't know it, but we've switched her rebellious daughter with a new, improved Christian one! Let's see if she notices a difference.

*(The Announcer exits and the action resumes.)*

**Mom:** Don't you look precious! Is it fifties day at school?

**Debbie:** No.

**Mom:** Where's your nose ring and belly shirt?

**Debbie:** I decided to dress more like a lady. You don't like it?

**Mom:** I love it!

**Debbie:** Thanks.

*(Dad walks in and sits.)*

**Dad:** Morning.

**Debbie:** Let me get your paper, Daddy. *(Debbie exits.)*

**Dad:** Who was that?

**Mom:** Debbie.

*(Dad laughs out loud, long and hard, slapping his leg.)*

**Dad:** That was a good one, honey. Debbie.

**Mom:** I'm not kidding.

*(Debbie returns, hands Dad the newspaper, gives him a kiss on the cheek, and sits. In shock Mom and Dad watch Debbie while she eats her breakfast.)*

**Dad:** Is everything OK, Debbie?

**Debbie:** Peachy! I mean, I'm a little concerned about my English test today, but I studied up for it over the weekend, so it'll be OK.

**Mom:** Peachy?

**Dad:** You studied on the weekend?

**Debbie:** Sure. Please pass the milk.

*(Mom passes the milk, dumbfounded.)*

**Mom:** Please?

**Dad:** All right, Debbie, how much?

**Debbie:** What?

**Dad:** What do you need money for? the prom? senior trip? Did you wreck the car? *(Dad jumps up and looks out an imaginary kitchen window.)*

**Debbie:** No, Dad! I don't need money. What's

wrong? Am I doing something wrong?

**Mom and Dad:** No!

*(Dad sits.)*

**Mom:** You're not doing anything wrong, honey. You're just a little…

**Dad:** Different.

**Mom:** But different is good. It's great!

**Dad:** You always said you liked being different.

**Mom:** And you're doing a great job of that right now.

**Debbie:** Good. *(Pause.)* I've got to motor. Don't want to be late! *(Debbie gives both of her parents a quick hug as she grabs her books and heads offstage.)*

**Debbie:** I love you two!

**Mom and Dad:** Love you.

*(Debbie runs back and grabs the apple from the table.)*

**Debbie:** For the teacher. Bye!

*(She exits. At a complete loss for words, Mom and Dad look at each other.)*

**Mom:** Who stole our daughter?

**Dad:** Who cares? I vote we keep this one.

*(The scene freezes, and the Announcer pops back onstage.)*

**Announcer:** Sure they noticed a difference, but who cares? You'll be so excited with the improvement, you'll never want to go back. Don't wait. Swap that hooligan teen for a Christian one today!

# Discussion Questions—Obeying Parents

- Do you ever feel like your parents want you to be like the new Debbie? Why or why not?

- What do you disagree with your parents about?

- Read aloud Proverbs 23:22. What is your duty to your parents? How does this apply to the areas in which you disagree?

- Do you have to be "boring" to be obedient? Why or why not?

- How can you respect your parents while maintaining your individuality?

- In what ways can you gain respect from your parents?

# Discussion Questions—Stereotypes

- How was Debbie a stereotype of a Christian teenager?

- What characteristics does the world perceive Christians to have? Which of these characteristics are true? Which are false?

- Read aloud John 13:34-35. What should Christians be known for? What does this look like?

- What prevents Christians from being known by love?

- How can we help change the incorrect perceptions and stereotypes people have of Christians?

# The Talking Mime

## Themes

- Hypocrisy (Matthew 23:23-25)
- Persecution (2 Timothy 3:12)

## The Cast

**Don:** Talk show host wearing a suit

**John:** Man dressed like a mime, wearing black clothes, his face painted white with dark lips and eyes (made with black lipstick and black eyeliner)

## The Setting:

A late-night talk show. To create this scene, place a desk and chair at stage left and angled toward the audience. Place a plush chair angled toward the desk.

## Props and Costumes:

A desk with a chair, a plush chair, a suit, black clothes, white face paint and makeup

## Media Option:

Use a theme song sound effect and a PowerPoint slide that reads, "Night Talk."

*Don is onstage sitting behind his desk. John is offstage.*

*Option: Display the* Night Talk *PowerPoint slide, and play the theme music to introduce the scene. Fade both during Don's opening speech.*

*The scene begins as Don starts speaking.*

**Don:** Welcome to *Night Talk*! I'm your host, Don Lake, and we have a very special guest for you today. You may assume a lot about him from his clothing, but don't judge the book by its cover! Please give a warm welcome to John Thompson!

*(Don stands and claps as John pulls himself onstage with an imaginary rope. John stops and waves to the audience. He shakes hands with Don and both sit down.)*

**Don:** We're so glad to have you on our show today, John.

*(John merely waves and smiles, but does not answer.)*

**Don:** Now correct me if I'm wrong, but you are a mime, right?

*(John mouths a response, but no sound comes out of his mouth.)*

**Don:** Excuse me?

*(John repeats his noiseless response, and then breaks into loud laughter.)*

**John:** I'm just messing with you, Don.

**Don:** You scared me there for a second.

**John:** Sorry, I couldn't help it. Yes, I'm a mime.

**Don:** But you are no ordinary mime, correct?

**John:** I think that's pretty obvious. When's the last time you had a conversation with a mime.

**Don:** Never.

**John:** Exactly. Mimes don't talk.

**Don:** But you do.

**John:** That's right, Don. I broke my vow of silence.

**Don:** Vow of silence?

**John:** It's a code that all mimes follow, like the Hippocratic oath doctors swear to before practicing medicine. We mimes also have a code, and one part of it is the vow of silence.

**Don:** How many other mimes have broken their silence?

**John:** None.

**Don:** You're the first.

**John:** I sure am.

**Don:** You seem proud of this.

**John:** I don't know about proud. More relieved that I can be myself, ya know? I don't have to live by somebody else's rules anymore.

**Don:** Why did you break your silence?

*(John stands and demonstrates his miming act, using his hands to indicate that he is trapped inside an invisible box.)*

**John:** I couldn't take it any more. There I am, out in the park like a good mime, just doing my job. Some people would stop and clap and enjoy my performance. Most would come up and heckle me, though.

**Don:** What do you mean?

**John:** They'd make fun of me! They'd get right in my face and yell stuff like, "Are you stupid? Can't you get out of the invisible box?" And little kids would always come over and try to play with me. They'd hit me and hide behind me, and I'd have to pretend like I didn't see them and search for 'em like a moron. Then people would yell, "Can't you find the kids, you stupid mime! They're right behind you!"

**Don:** How long did this go on for?

**John:** About four days before I finally cracked. This guy kept going on and on saying, "Pretend it's really windy. Come on, walk against the wind." I got right in his face and yelled, "It's so windy because you keep opening your big fat mouth!" It freaked him out so bad that he fainted.

**Don:** Why did you want to be a mime in the first place?

**John:** I always loved seeing mimes when I was a kid! They always seemed so happy, and they made me laugh. While I was attending the School of Mime, no one ever told me about how bad your feet hurt and how

jerky people could be.

**Don:** Why do you still wear that outfit if you're not a mime anymore?

**John:** I'm still a mime.

**Don:** But you said mimes don't talk, and you're talking quite a bit.

**John:** Look, I graduated from the School of Mime. My diploma's on the wall. I'm still a mime even if I don't act like one.

**Don:** But you're just like me if you talk.

**John:** Hey, as long as I look like a mime, what's the difference? I mean, I say I'm a mime. I dress like a mime. People look at me and think I'm a mime. In my book, that makes me a mime.

**Don:** *(Turning toward the audience)* There you have it, the secret world of mimedom revealed by an insider. Thank you for being on the show today, Mr. Thompson.

**John:** My pleasure, Don.

**Don:** We've got to take a break. We'll be right back with Chef Be-Be and her amazing slug soufflés, so stick around for more *Night Talk*!

*(Option: The* Night Talk *slide and theme music come back up as the stage lights go to black.)*

# Discussion Questions—Hypocrisy

- Do you think the mime was a hypocrite? Why or why not?

- Are there any famous people who you think are hypocrites? Who and why?

- What do you think these people would look like if their outside appearances matched their insides?

- Read aloud Matthew 23:23-25. Why do you think Jesus hates hypocrisy so much?

- Do you have areas of hypocrisy in your life? If yes, how can you change them?

- How can you guard yourself against becoming hypocritical?

# Discussion Questions—Persecution

- How did the ridicule the mime endured during his performance in the park affect his outlook on life?

- Have you ever been ridiculed for your beliefs? If yes, how did it affect you?

- Do you think you could be pressured into denying your faith? Why or why not?

- Read aloud 2 Timothy 3:12. What are some examples of Christians being persecuted in your school? in your community? around the world?

- How can we help Christians around the world who are persecuted for their faith?

- How can we take advantage of our right to openly share our faith?

# Use Your Legs

## Themes

- Relying on God (John 15:5)
- Pride (Proverbs 16:18)

## The Cast

**Bud:** Blue-collar worker, wearing work clothes (jeans and a T-shirt) and a wristwatch

**Rod:** Blue-collar worker, wearing work clothes (jeans and a T-shirt)

**Superman:** The traditional superhero, wearing his Superman cape with a Hawaiian shirt, shorts, sunglasses, and a Superman S on his chest

## The Setting:

Outdoors. At stage right, place a lawn chair for Superman and angle it toward the audience. Place a cardboard box on the ground at stage left.

## Props and Costumes:

A large empty box, a newspaper, lawn chair, clipboard with paper on it, a glass of lemonade, two sets of work clothes, a wristwatch, a Superman cape, Hawaiian shirt, shorts, sunglasses, a Superman S made out of paper or fabric

*Superman is onstage, sitting in the lawn chair reading the newspaper and drinking lemonade. Bud and Rod are offstage.*

*The scene begins as Bud and Rod enter from stage left and survey the cardboard box. Rod carries the clipboard.*

**Bud:** What do ya think?

**Rod:** Doesn't look bad.

**Bud:** You sure this is the right one? Remember we moved the wrong house that one time.

**Rod:** Were the Johnsons freaked when they got home. *(Pulls out the clipboard and looks at the attached paperwork.)* Says right here this is it.

**Bud:** What's in it?

**Rod:** Doesn't say.

**Bud:** *(To Superman)* Hey, buddy!

*(Superman lowers his newspaper.)*

**Superman:** Me?

**Bud:** Yeah, you. You know what's in here?

*(Superman squints his eyes and uses his X-ray vision. He returns to his paper.)*

**Superman:** Looks like a tractor engine.

**Rod:** You hear that?

**Bud:** This is a back breaker all right.

**Rod:** Not that! He said, "looks like." He saw what's inside. *(Thinks.)* I think he's Superman.

**Bud:** Superman?! Couldn't be. We're a thousand miles from Metropolis.

**Rod:** He's got a cape, Bud.

*(Bud stares at the man who, with the S symbol on his chest and cape on his back, is obviously Superman.)*

**Bud:** You might be right. *(Bud walks up to Superman and taps his newspaper.)* 'Scuse me, sir?

*(Superman lowers his newspaper.)*

**Superman:** Yes?

**Bud:** My friend and I…

**Rod:** *(Waves.)* I'm Rod.

**Bud:** We were wondering, well…

**Superman:** Yes, I am.

**Rod:** You can read minds, too?

**Superman:** I heard you two talking. Superhearing, remember?

**Rod:** Oh yeah.

**Bud:** It's a pleasure to meet you.

**Superman:** I'm just here to serve.

*(Superman holds his hand out to shake. Bud takes it and shakes. Superman pulls his hand away, groaning as if Bud's grip hurt his hand.)*

**Bud:** I'm so sorry!

**Superman:** Gotcha! *(Laughs.)* Just a joke. I'm fine.

**Bud:** Right. Well, nice to meet you, sir. Have a nice day!

**Superman:** I will. I'm on vacation.

**Rod:** Stay out of trouble!

(Superman returns to his newspaper while Bud and Rod run excitedly back over to stage left.)

**Bud:** Can you believe it? It's really him!

**Rod:** They'll never believe us back at the office. We should get a picture.

**Bud:** I don't think he shows up on film. Or is that Dracula? *(Looks at his watch.)* We better get moving.

**Rod:** Let's load up and split.

*(Both men position themselves on either side of the box.)*

**Rod:** One…

**Bud:** Two…

**Both:** Three!

*(Both strain. The box doesn't budge. Exhausted, Bud and Rod stop.)*

**Rod:** It weighs a ton!

**Bud:** Use your legs.

**Rod:** I was using everything!

**Bud:** We're smarter than a dumb box. Come on.

*(They again position themselves to lift the box.)*

**Rod:** One…

**Bud:** Two…

**Both:** Three!

*(They struggle and strain twice as long this time. Nothing happens, and they fall away from the box, spent.)*

**Bud:** It moved that time.

**Rod:** My arms moved out of their sockets, that's for sure.

**Bud:** We'll never move it.

**Rod:** Maybe Superman could give us a hand.

**Bud:** You kidding? He's on vacation. Besides, we can do it ourselves.

**Rod:** What's it hurt to ask?

**Bud:** He's been saving the world from destruction! He's got more important things to do than move a box. Are you gonna help?

**Rod:** I guess.

**Bud:** Let's get on the same side. Maybe we can tilt it up.

**Rod:** Whatever.

*(They crouch side by side, gripping the box and prepare to lift it.)*

**Rod:** One…

**Bud:** Two…

**Both:** Three!

*(They strain, and the box moves an inch or so.)*

**Bud:** *(Through clenched teeth)* Almost there!

**Rod:** Can't hold…

*(Rod loses his grip, and the box falls on Bud's foot.)*

**Bud:** Owww!!!

**Rod:** Are you OK?

**Bud:** *(In extreme pain)* Box…on…foot!

**Superman:** *Can I help?*

**Rod:** Yes, please...

**Bud:** *(Sternly)* No! I'm fine.

**Superman:** *(Not convinced)* I'm right here if you need any help. *(Superman returns to his paper.)*

**Rod:** Bud!

**Bud:** Pull.

*(Both men grab Bud's trapped foot. Finally, it comes free. Bud gasps in relief, massaging his foot.)*

**Rod:** You OK?

**Bud:** I'm going home.

**Rod:** What about the job?

**Bud:** We'll do it later. Help me to the truck.

**Rod:** Sure.

*(Rod helps Bud limp off the stage. Superman watches them exit. He puts down his paper and walks over to the box.)*

**Superman:** Just ask, guys. *(Superman bends down and picks up the box as if it were a feather. He walks offstage with it.)*

# Discussion Questions—Relying on God

- Have you ever tried to do something by yourself that you needed help with? What happened?

- Is it possible to rely on God in every aspect of your life? Why or why not?

- Read aloud John 15:5. What can you do without God's help?

- Why do we try to do things without God's help when he's willing to help?

- What activities do you regularly do without relying on God?

- How would involving God in them change your life?

# Discussion Questions—Pride

- Why didn't Bud want Superman's help?

- Has pride ever prevented you from asking for help? What happened?

- Read aloud Proverbs 16:18. Why is pride so dangerous?

- What is the difference between pride and confidence?

- Which of your skills or talents do you have the most confidence in?

- What steps can you take to protect yourself from pride?

# Topical Index

Absolute Truth . . . . . . . . . . . . . . . . . . . . .44

Bible Study . . . . . . . . . . . . . . . . . . . . . .53

Christlikeness . . . . . . . . . . . . . . . . . . . .15

Christmas . . . . . . . . . . . . . . . . . . . . . .73

Devotion to Christ . . . . . . . . . . . . . . . . .19

Facing Temptation . . . . . . . . . . . . . . . . .64

Focus . . . . . . . . . . . . . . . . . . . . . . . . .77

Following God's Will . . . . . . . . . . . . . . . .68

Forgiveness . . . . . . . . . . . . . . . . . . . . .27

God's Love . . . . . . . . . . . . . . . . . . . . . .30

God's Sovereignty . . . . . . . . . . . . . . . . .11

Gossip . . . . . . . . . . . . . . . . . . . . . . . .60

Hearing God . . . . . . . . . . . . . . . . . . . . .57

Heaven . . . . . . . . . . . . . . . . . . . . . . . .53

Hypocrisy . . . . . . . . . . . . . . . . . . . . . .85

Impure Motives . . . . . . . . . . . . . . . . . . .57

Integrity . . . . . . . . . . . . . . . . . . . . . . .39

Judging . . . . . . . . . . . . . . . . . . . . . . . .49

Media Influence . . . . . . . . . . . . . . . . . . .23

New Life . . . . . . . . . . . . . . . . . . . . . . . .15

Obeying Parents . . . . . . . . . . . . . . . . . .81

Peer Pressure . . . . . . . . . . . . . . . . . . . .39

Persecution . . . . . . . . . . . . . . . . . . . . .85

Premarital Sex . . . . . . . . . . . . . . . . . . . .64

Pride . . . . . . . . . . . . . . . . . . . . . . . . . .89

Racism and Prejudice . . . . . . . . . . . . . . .49

Relevance of the Bible . . . . . . . . . . . . . . .34

Relying on God . . . . . . . . . . . . . . . . . . .89

Responsibility . . . . . . . . . . . . . . . . . . . .23

Sacrifice . . . . . . . . . . . . . . . . . . . . . . .68

Salvation . . . . . . . . . . . . . . . . . . . . . . .34

Sharing Your Faith . . . . . . . . . . . . . . . . .44

Sin . . . . . . . . . . . . . . . . . . . . . . . . . . .19

Stereotypes . . . . . . . . . . . . . . . . . . . . .81

Submitting to Others . . . . . . . . . . . . . . . .11

Talents . . . . . . . . . . . . . . . . . . . . . . . .77

Thanksgiving . . . . . . . . . . . . . . . . . . . . .30

Trust . . . . . . . . . . . . . . . . . . . . . . . . . .60

Urgency of Following Christ . . . . . . . . . . .73

Violence . . . . . . . . . . . . . . . . . . . . . . . .27

# Scripture Index

Genesis 4:3-8 . . . . . . . . . . . . . . . . . . . . .27

1 Chronicles 29:11-13 . . . . . . . . . . . . . .11

Psalm 107:8-9 . . . . . . . . . . . . . . . . . . . .30

Psalm 119:105-106 . . . . . . . . . . . . . . . .53

Psalm 119:129-130 . . . . . . . . . . . . . . . .34

Proverbs 16:18 . . . . . . . . . . . . . . . . . . .89

Proverbs 16:27-28 . . . . . . . . . . . . . . . . .60

Proverbs 23:22 . . . . . . . . . . . . . . . . . . .81

Proverbs 25:19 . . . . . . . . . . . . . . . . . . .60

Isaiah 55:6-7 . . . . . . . . . . . . . . . . . . . . .73

Jeremiah 2:11-13 . . . . . . . . . . . . . . . . . .19

Jeremiah 33:3 . . . . . . . . . . . . . . . . . . . .57

Ezekiel 18:20-22 . . . . . . . . . . . . . . . . . .23

Amos 5:10 . . . . . . . . . . . . . . . . . . . . . . .39

Matthew 7:1-2 . . . . . . . . . . . . . . . . . . . .49

Matthew 18:21-35 . . . . . . . . . . . . . . . . .27

Matthew 22:35-40 . . . . . . . . . . . . . . . . .68

Matthew 23:23-25 . . . . . . . . . . . . . . . . .85

Luke 2:1-7 . . . . . . . . . . . . . . . . . . . . . . .73

John 13:34-35 . . . . . . . . . . . . . . . . . . . .81

John 14:1-4 . . . . . . . . . . . . . . . . . . . . . .53

John 15:5 . . . . . . . . . . . . . . . . . . . . . . . .89

Acts 5:1-11 . . . . . . . . . . . . . . . . . . . . . .57

Acts 9:10-27 . . . . . . . . . . . . . . . . . . . . .15

Romans 5:6-9 . . . . . . . . . . . . . . . . . . . .30

Romans 6:1-2 . . . . . . . . . . . . . . . . . . . .19

1 Corinthians 6:18-20 . . . . . . . . . . . . . .64

1 Corinthians 10:12-13 . . . . . . . . . . . . .39

2 Corinthians 5:14-15 . . . . . . . . . . . . . .34

2 Corinthians 10:3-5 . . . . . . . . . . . . . . .23

Galatians 3:27-29 . . . . . . . . . . . . . . . . .49

Ephesians 5:1-6 . . . . . . . . . . . . . . . . . . .15

Colossians 3:17 . . . . . . . . . . . . . . . . . . .77

2 Timothy 3:12 . . . . . . . . . . . . . . . . . . .85

Hebrews 13:17 . . . . . . . . . . . . . . . . . . .11

James 1:14-16 . . . . . . . . . . . . . . . . . . . .64

1 Peter 3:14-16 . . . . . . . . . . . . . . . . . . .44

1 John 2:15-17 . . . . . . . . . . . . . . . . . . .77

1 John 3:16 . . . . . . . . . . . . . . . . . . . . . .68

3 John 2-4 . . . . . . . . . . . . . . . . . . . . . . .44

Group Publishing, Inc.
Attention: Product Development
P.O. Box 481
Loveland, CO 80539
Fax: (970) 679-4370

## Evaluation for
## *Ultimate Skits*

Please help Group Publishing, Inc. continue to provide innovative and useful resources for ministry. Please take a moment to fill out this evaluation and mail or fax it to us. Thanks!

● ● ●

1. As a whole, this book has been (circle one)

not very helpful                                          very helpful

1     2     3     4     5     6     7     8     9     10

2. The best things about this book:

3. Ways this book could be improved:

4. Things I will change because of this book:

5. Other books I'd like to see Group publish in the future:

6. Would you be interested in field-testing future Group products and giving us your feedback? If so, please fill in the information below:

Name _____

Church Name _____

Denomination _____ Church Size _____

Church Address _____

City _____ State _____ ZIP _____

Church Phone _____

E-mail _____

# Grab Students' Hearts and Go Deeper!

## Group's BlockBuster Movie Illustrations: Over 160 Clips for Your Ministry!

*Bryan Belknap*

**You have to "PLAY" for your students' attention!**

Want to change students' lives? Just press "play." Now you can use popular movies to illustrate what the Bible has to say about the critical issues teenagers face. Each clip includes "where-you-live" discussion questions to get youth talking! The convenient Scripture and theme indexes make finding the right illustration easy! Plus, by teaching with a medium that teenagers relate to, you'll be keeping your ministry relevant.

**ISBN 0-7644-2256-1**

## The Top 20 Messages for Youth Ministry

*Jim Kochenburger*

**Complete, cutting-edge messages your youth group will never forget!**

No matter what your speaking ability, you'll find what you need in *The Top 20 Messages for Youth Ministry*. This incredibly useful resource contains 20 complete, power-packed message outlines to slice and dice and make your own. Featuring: clear, topical outlines with Bible-based points; over 20 great stories and illustrations; more than 20 great movie clip illustration ideas; over 50 quick and easy ideas for involving group members in your message, and a boatload of extra ideas! Take your speaking to the next level with *The Top Twenty Messages for Youth Ministry*.

**ISBN 0-7644-2258-8**

## Hilarious Skits for Youth Ministry

*Chris Chapman*

Easy-to-act and fun-to-watch, these 8 youth group skits are guaranteed to get your kids laughing and listening. These skits help your kids discover spiritual truths! Skits last from 5 to 15 minutes, so there's a skit to fit into any program!

**ISBN 0-7644-2033-X**

## Hilarious Skits for Youth Ministry 2

*Chris and Sue Chapman*

These 10 truly laugh-out-loud skits teach the Bible and captivate kids every time they're performed! Use them as discussion starters, learning tools, entertainment, or even full-scale productions...all guaranteed to tickle the funny bone and drive home spiritual truths. Involve everyone with tiny bit parts, in-between parts or long speaking roles. Youth workers can find something for each of their kids to do! Even the most hesitant teenagers will be laughing, learning and having a good time.

**ISBN 0-7644-2185-9**

## An Unstoppable Force: Daring to Become the Church God Had in Mind

*Erwin McManus*

Be inspired about being part of the Church God had in mind—a "force" created to change the world. A Church free from atrophied practices, flourishing in creative and compelling worship, reaching out to the community with "outside the box" expressions of love and faith. (hardcover)

**ISBN 0-7644-2306-1**